I0343626

A Description of the Prayers by Patriarch Ignatius Bar Wahib

Texts from Christian Late Antiquity

70

Series Editor

George Anton Kiraz

TeCLA (Texts from Christian Late Antiquity) is a series presenting ancient Christian texts both in their original languages and with accompanying contemporary English translations.

A Description of the Prayers by Patriarch Ignatius Bar Wahib

Edited and Translated by

Fr. Baby Varghese

Gorgias Press

2022

Gorgias Press LLC, 954 River Road, Piscataway, NJ, 08854, USA

www.gorgiaspress.com

Copyright © 2022 by Gorgias Press LLC

All rights reserved under International and Pan-American Copyright Conventions. No part of this publication may be reproduced, stored in a retrieval system or transmitted in any form or by any means, electronic, mechanical, photocopying, recording, scanning or otherwise without the prior written permission of Gorgias Press LLC.

2022

ISBN 978-1-4632-4404-0 **ISSN 1935-6846**

Library of Congress Cataloging-in-Publication Data

A Cataloging-in-Publication Record is available at the Library of Congress.

Printed in the United States of America

TABLE OF CONTENTS

INTRODUCTION

We have very little information about the life of Ignatius Bar Wahib [Badr Zakkai or Zokhe], Patriarch of Mardin. The main source of information is the *Ecclesiastical Chronicle* by Bar Hebraeus. An unknown author who continued the Chronicle gives a brief narrative.[1] Zokhe or Joseph Badr al-Din son of Ibrahim, known as Bar Wahib, became the patriarch of Mardin in 1293 and led the Syrian Orthodox Church for forty years (1293–1333). Two shorter narratives are given by the Supplement to the Chronicle[2] and in *Bibliotheca Orientalis*.[3]

Though he was installed as the rival patriarch, one of the two other claimants soon passed away and Bar Wahib remained in office for 40 years. The popular Maphrian Bar Hebraeus Bar-

---

[1] J.B. Abbeloos and T.J. Lamy (ed.), *Gregori Barhebraei Chronicon Ecclesiasticum* (Louvain, 1872, pp. 781–791; Syr. and Eng. Tr. David Wilmshurst, *Bar Hebraeus, The Ecclesiastical Chronicle*, (Gorgias Press, Piscataway, NJ, 2016), pp. 282–286.

[2] J.B. Abbeloos & T.J. Lamy, op. cit., pp. 907–912; cfr. 496; Wilmshurst, op. cit. pp. 478–480. Syriac texts from Barhebraeus are given by Rifaat Ebied & Archbishop Malki Malki in an appendix: "Patriarch Ignatius Bar Wahib's (d.1333) Treatise on the Six Syriac Letters that have Two Sounds", *THE HARP* 32 (2017), pp. 9–33; here pp. 29–33.

[3] Joseph Assemanus, *Bibliotheca Orientalis Clementino Vaticana*, t. II (Rome, 1721), pp. 381–382; 464–465. See also Ignatius Aphram I Barsoum, *The History of Syriac Literature and Sciences* (tr. Matti Moosa, Peublo, 2000), p. 161; 229; also Rifaat Ebied & Malki Malki, art. cit. p. 10.

soum al-Safi (1288–1308), younger brother of Bar Hebraeus the Great, supported Ignatius Mikha'il I as the legitimate patriarch, but Bar Wahib used his political influence and diplomacy to gain recognition from Barsoum al-Safi. David Wilmshurst's translation of the narration of these events is given below:[4]

> "After Philoxenos [Nemrud: 1283–1292], three illegitimate patriarchs: firstly Constantine of Melitene [Ignatius Constantine, 1292–93], secondly Barsawma, the archimandrite of Gawikath [Ignatius Mikhai'l, 1292–1312], and thirdly Badr Zakkai of Mardin [Ignatius V bar Wahib, 1293–1333].
>
> After Philoxenos died in the monastery of Mar Barsawma, the patriarchate was illegitimately seized in the beginning of the year 1604 of the Greeks [AD 1292/93] by three men who behaved like bandits. One of these was Constantine, who was not fit to hold any of the grades of the priesthood. This man, who was metropolitan of Melitene in name only, seized the patriarchate by bribery. He assembled three bishops from the vicinity, who consecrated him patriarch.
>
> The second was the archimandrite of Gawikath [in Cilicia], the same man who failed to win support for his own bid before the consecration of the previous patriarch. The bishops of the West rallied around him because he was well in with the king of Armenia and with the Mongols and Greeks in many regions, and they proclaimed him patriarch of all the West, and established his throne in the monastery of Gawikath. His name was Mikha'il, and they called him Ignatius. He was also proclaimed by Bar Hebraeus II in the East and in the West; though Bar Hebraeus Barsawma al-Safi fled to Maragha, Adarbaigan and Tabriz, where he remained for five years, so as not to receive Bar Wahib, who had been consecrated after two other patriarchs. Finally, the third was Bar Wahib Badr Zakkai, of Mardin, from a family of Tur 'Abdin, who sprang from the village of Gurnasha near the for-

[4] Wilmshurst, pp. 282–284. Abbellos & Lamy, pp. 781–787.

tress of Maytam. He assembled three or four of the bishops of Tur 'Abdin, and they proclaimed him patriarch out of fear of the sultan of the Hagarenes, at least for Mardin and Tur 'Abdin. Since the name of patriarch had been besmirched, they called him Ignatius as well. [......].

Then both the West and the East persisted for five years in proclaiming the Westerner Mikha'il of Cilicia, namely Rabban Barsawma, the superior of Gawikath. The people of Tur 'Abdin and Mardin responded by proclaiming Bar Wahib. But Bar Wahib, seeing himself neglected and not proclaimed in the east, was offended and greatly saddened, and went up to Malik al-Mansur, the lord of Mardin, and bribed him with presents. He explained to him how a patriarch was elected, and said that he would only be regarded as a legitimate patriarch if his name was proclaimed in the East by the maphrian. The sultan granted his petition, and sent one of his own messengers to announce his decision. The patriarch also sent one of his disciples, who carried the sultan's rescript and a humble letter from the patriarch himself, together with gifts that befitted the fathers. They set out to find the maphrian Barsawma, who was keeping the vigil at the tomb of his brother Bar Hebraeus in Maragha; but he turned them away, so that they returned in failure. But a little later Bar Hebraeus [al-Safi] thought over the matter, and said: 'I will arise in the Church and dissension should be stirred up on that account'. And so he set out, and came to the monastery of Mar Mattai, where he was greeted with honour (as he was everywhere else in the East). Then he went up to the monastery of Mar Daniel, known as 'Beetles'.[5]

While he was staying there, the two messengers from the sultan of Mardin and the patriarch again came to see him, bearing letters and gifts. This time the maphrian gave him a friendly welcome and in their presence conceded the patriar-

[5] 'Beetles': *habshushyatha*.

chate, in the usual form, to Bar Wahib Badr Zakkai, in accordance with the wishes of the lord of Mosul. When the messengers returned, those who had sent them rejoiced greatly; for the maphrian had written a letter of institution, and committed the throne to the patriarch.

After all this disturbance had ended, the maphrian Bar Hebraeus Barsauma Safi died in the year 1619 [AD 1308]. The East remained widowed of its shepherd for the space of nine years, because it was at that time impossible for the patriarch to consecrate a maphrian, because he was afraid that they would not receive him. In the year 1628 [AD 1317], however, the Easterners were forced to go to the patriarch, so that he might consecrate a maphrian for them. Because the roads were cut, and because of the frequent quarrels between the rulers, they were unable to reach the patriarch of Cilicia, so they went instead to the Mardin patriarch Bar Wahib. He consecrated for them Rabban Mattai bar Hnanu from the monastery of Mar Mattai, and named him Gregory.[6] Now the Westerners, Easterners and Northerners had already hastened to proclaim a patriarch of Cilicia; and the Easterners and the people of Tur 'Abdin were also proclaiming a patriarch of Mardin; and so the maphrian Barsawma Safi Bar Hebraeus had recognized them both, first the patriarch of Cilicia and then the patriarch of Mardin. [....].

Bar Zakkai died in the monastery of Mar Hnanya near Mardin in the year 1644 [AD 1333], in the week of the Lord's Passion, after fulfilling his office for forty years. He was a most talented student of religion and philosophy, who wielded great influence with the rulers. He explained the alphabet in Syriac and Arabic and left a most joyful anaphora in the Church".[7]

---

[6] Maphrian Gregory Mattai (1317–1345).

[7] His treatise on the alphabet has been edited by Ebied & Malki Malki. See above, note 2. The Anaphora is edited with an English translation:

Though the author of the Chronicle refers to him as "most talented student of religion and philosophy", he was rather an ambitious prelate for higher position in the Church, who would use every possible means to get it.

The present volume provides an edition of Bar Wahib's "Description of the Prayers" from a manuscript of the Orthodox Theological Seminary, Kottayam (No. 211; Old No. 20), copied in 1915 from a manuscript of the Konat Library. Patriarch Aphaim Barsoum refers to two other manuscripts ("MS at our library and Birmingham MS 100").[8] The treatise is not particularly original in its content and it does not discuss the history or the theology of the canonical hours. It is rather a description of the externals of the prayers. One can observe traces of the influence of the Arabic language. The regulations on washing are reminiscent of Islamic customs.

The regulations regarding prostrations probably represent the custom followed in Mardin. In fact, in the Syrian Orthodox Church rubrics and liturgical customs were not always uniform.

An extract from this treatise (in Syriac) was quoted in the introduction to the *Book of Common Prayer* (Shehimo) (Fr. Abraham Konat, ed., *Ktobo d-slutho shhimto*, Pampakuda, 1968, 3rd. edition). Here, I offer the complete text with an English translation for the first time. My sincere thanks to Dr. Sebastian Brock, who has kindly corrected my translation and suggested a number of corrections in the Syriac text. However, I am solely responsible for any errors or printing mistakes in the Syriac or English text that remain. My sincere thanks to Dr. George Kiraz for accepting the text for publication and also to Dr. Melonie Schmierer-Lee, for her commendable skills in editing the text.

B. Varghese, *Order of the Anaphoras*, MOC Publications, Kottayam, 2021), pp. 178–207. [From ms. Cambridge 2887]. For other literary works of Bar Wahib, see: Ignatius Aphraim Barsoum, p. 161.

[8] Ignatius Apraim Barsoum, p. 229, n. 21. The Mingana manuscript is indeed Mingana Syr. 100D; the text is also found in Mingana Syr. 87A.

GLOSSARY OF TERMS

Bo'utho (pl: *Bo'wotho*)	Supplication; a hymn sung at the end of an office.
'edono	Time; nocturn.
'enyono	Antiphon; anthem; response sung between the verses of a Psalm.
'eqbo	A hymn sung at the conclusion of a series of Psalms.
Hulolo	Versicle of a Psalm or a Biblical Ode sung before the Gospel.
Lilyo	Night Prayer.
m'irono	Nocturn; Vigil; opening part of *Lilyo*
pethgomo	Versicle from the Psalm sung before a *qolo*.
Promiun	From Greek *Prooimion*; Introduction to a prayer called *Sedro*.
Qolo (pl: *qole*)	A hymn.
Qudosh 'edtho	Consecration of the Church; first Sunday of the Liturgical Year.
Ramsho	Evening; Vespers..
Sapro	Morning; morning prayer.
Sedro (pl: *Sedre*)	A long prayer preceded by *promiun*.
Sutoro	Compline.
Qonuno	From Greek kanon; a hymn.
Quqliun	Cycle of hymns beginning with verses from the Psalms.
Qurbono	Offering; the Eucharistic liturgy.
Qnuma (pl; *Qnume*)	Hypostasis.
Takshaptho	Supplication; a hymn.

TEXT AND TRANSLATION

A DESCRIPTION OF THE PRAYERS BY PATRIARCH IGNATIUS BAR WAHIB (+1333)

1. [Trusting] in the power of the Holy Trinity, Consubstantial, Father, Son and the Holy Spirit, we write the regulation concerning the prayers of the Church, and on their numbers and the prostrations (*segdotho*) that are done in them. From the mysteries hidden in the divine writings and from the exposition of the former doctors (for) the illumination of the hearts of those who desire the light of the divine knowledge.

It was composed by our father Patriarch Mor Ignatius Bar Wahib. May his prayer protect the steadfast reader and the hearer having discernment as well as the weak scribe. Amen.

2. Those who are set apart and called to the spiritual ministry of the Holy Trinity, from the womb of baptism, the mother who bears spiritual children to the heavenly Father, born and chosen to be brethren to His Only Begotten Son, because of Incarnation, and were called and counted and held worthy and perfected to be participants of the Holy Spirit by His descent upon the Holy Apostles, ought to follow carefully, and consider with understanding and perception the hidden mysteries of the Holy Church, and their ordering and the setting out of their laws, especially and particularly the regulations of prayers and their ordering. **[2]**[1] in the precise and established times (*'edone*), and about the prostrations (*segdotho*) in the prayers and their numbers and quantity, that were established and prescribed by the Holy Apostles and by the blessed former fathers.

---

[1] The page number of the manuscript is provided here.

1. ܥܠ ܚܝܠܐ ܕܐܠܗܘܬܐ ܩܕܝܫܬܐ ܫܘܪܝ ܟܬܘܒܐ. ܐܬܐ ܘܟܒܪ ܘܙܘܥܐ
ܩܕܝܫܐ ܠܡܠܦܢ ܐܡܘܪܐ ܕܒܘܟܪܬܐ ܕܒܐܬܪܬܐ ܘܫܬܝܢܝܢ ܟܡ ܫܢܝܬܐ ܕܒܗܘܢ
ܡܬܠܡܕܝܢ. ܡܢ ܙܒܢܐ ܕܒܗܘܢ ܒܦܘܠܚܢܐ ܠܐܠܗܐ ܘܡܢ ܫܡܫܐ ܡܠܦܢܐ ܩܕܝܫܐ
ܡܫܘܕܥܢܐ ܕܟܬܒܬܐ ܘܐܝܟܢ ܕܟܘܠ ܢܘܗܪܐ ܘܢܘܟܪܝܐ ܠܐܠܗܘܬܐ ܫܡܝܢ.
ܕܟܝܢ ܠܐܟܘܢ ܦܩܘܪܘ ܡܢܗ ܐܝܟܢܐܝܬ ܕܗܘ ܒܪܘܚܐ. ܕܟܠܗ
ܠܐܢܫ ܒܦܪܘܫܐ ܠܐܝܕܐ ܘܒܡܫܡܫܢܐ ܦܪܘܫܐ ܘܒܫܘܠܡܐ ܡܫܝܚܐ ܐܡܝܢ ❖

2. ܕܝܢ ܠܐܠܗܐ ܕܒܫܡܫܬܐ ܘܡܫܝܚܐ ܕܐܠܗܘܬܐ ܩܕܝܫܬܐ ܠܐܦܪܣ
ܘܐܬܦܪܣ ܡܢ ܒܪܫܐ ܕܡܫܡܫܢܘܬܐ ܐܬܐ ܕܟܕ ܒܢܝܐ ܪܘܚܐ ܠܐܬܦܫܛܐ
ܐܠܐܟܝܢ. ܘܐܬܟܢܫܘ. ܘܐܡܪܐ ܠܡܫܡܫܢܐ ܒܪܐ ܕܝܠܗ. ܒܟܠܗ ܡܢ ܦܫܝܛܘܬܐ
ܐܠܗܘܬܐ ܘܐܬܡܢܥ. ܘܡܩܦܐ ܠܒܘܫܐ ܩܕܝܫܐ ܒܡܫܟܢܗ ܘܟܠ ܡܫܝܚܐ
ܩܕܝܫܐ ܐܠܗܘܬ ܘܐܠܗܘܬܗ. ܕܝܠܗ ܢܗܝܪܘܬܐ. ܘܠܗ ܡܫܡܫܢܘܬܗ
ܘܡܠܦܢܘܬܗ ܥܠ ܙܘܙܐ ܒܦܘܡܐ ܕܒܪܬܐ ܩܕܝܫܬܐ ܘܒܠ ܬܫܒܘܚܬܐ ܘܫܘܒܚܐ
ܢܣܒܘܢܝܗ. ܘܐܠܗܘܬܗ ܘܡܫܡܫܢܘܬܗ ܥܠ ܐܡܘܪܐ ܕܒܘܟܪܬܐ ܘܬܫܒܘܚܬܐ
ܕܟܝܢ *[2] ܒܢܝܐ ܢܩܝܐ ܘܩܕܝܫܐ. ܘܡܫܡܫܢܝܬܐ ܕܒܪܬܐ ܘܫܬܝܢܝܢ
ܘܡܫܬܡܠܝܢ. ܐܝܟܢ ܕܡܢ ܡܫܝܚܐ ܩܕܝܫܐ. ܘܡܢ ܐܦܘܬܐ ܬܫܒܘܚܬܐ ܩܕܝܫܐ
ܐܬܐܦܝܣ ܘܐܬܩܕܫ

[2] Star (*) denotes the beginning of a new page. The page number is given in the English text.

3. Over the course of times, seasons, years and generations they were handed over and came down to us, and the prayers become weak and altered while the prostrations (*segdotho*) were reduced and changed to the point when our lot sounded out (?) and the end of time had reached us. Then by the surging of the ocean of thoughts, we were tossed and by the waves of reflections, we were ruined and drowned, for we see the orderings are disregarded and the regulations are altered and (even) suppressed, and all the children of the Church adhere to their own ways to which they are accustomed. And they follow their own course, acting heedlessly and negligently and without understanding. There are many who make several prostrations (*segdotho*) and even more (than required) at the time of the prayers and others do not make any prostrations at all. Others make three prostrations with each prayer and say it is enough. Others (make) five, six or more or even less.

4. Everyone without any clear knowledge kneels down (*brek*) and prostrates (*sged*) in different ways and with disorder, and thinks that he is building upon the foundation of truth. [p. 3] Then we raised our eyes towards God who orders everything, and we beseeched that we could make an examination of the issue. Immediately the divine grace spread its wings over our feebleness and showered forth its mercies upon our feebleness, telling us to enter the ocean of divine writings, for in them, we will find the mysteries of the divine knowledge that we seek. We beseeched the same grace from which (proceeds) every good thing, to grant us facility of speech [lit: opening of our mouth] in the matter with which we are engaged, even though we are too feeble for our quest to be fittingly fulfilled, nor are we worthy. Let us offer unceasing glory to the Holy Trinity who gives us what is good and perfects spiritual gifts for us who are (so) deficient.

3. ܘܒܗ ܫܘܠܛܢܐ ܕܪ̈ܫܐ ܘܕܝ̈ܢܐ ܘܥܡ̈ܡܐ ܘܢܘܪܐ ܐܬܟܢܫܘ ܘܐܬܟܢ̈ܫܘ. ܘܙܒ̈ܢܐ
ܐܬܪܦ ܘܐܬܟܢܫܘ. ܘܣܓܝ̈ܐܐ ܐܬܦܪܩܘ ܘܐܬܟܢܫܘ. ܕܝܢܐ ܕܫܡܥܘ ܐܬܐܡܪ
ܘܡܛܠܬܗܘܢ ܕܪ̈ܫܐ ܠܒܝܬ ܡܠܟܘܬܐ. ܗܝܕܝܢ ܒܡܣܡ̈ܪܐ ܐܝܟ ܚܘ̈ܛܪܐ ܐܬܦܪܣܘ.
ܘܒܟܠܗ ܕܘ̈ܝܐ ܐܬܡܚܝܘ ܐܬܕܝܢܘ. ܕܢܣܒܘ ܠܛܘܒܥܐ ܘܐܬܬܠܝܘ. ܘܒܥܠܡ̈ܬܩܠܐ
ܘܐܬܠܚܡܘ ܘܐܬܟܠܠܘ. ܘܒܗܘܢ ܒܢ̈ܝ ܚܝܐ ܠܐܘܪܚܐ ܕܢܦܩܐ ܢܦܫܗ
ܘܐܬܟܠܠܘ. ܘܒܐܬܪܗܘܢ ܕܫܠܐ ܪܘܚܗܘܢ ܘܠܐ ܚܝܝܢ. ܘܐܝܟ ܙ̈ܐܬܐ ܘܟܡ̈ܘܟܐ
ܚ̈ܒܝܢ ܘܠܐ ܡܫܬܠܛܝܢ. ܘܐܝܠ ܒܗܘܢ ܡܛ̈ܐܬܐ ܒܒܝܬ ܙܟܘ̈ܬܐ ܡܛܝ̈ܒܬܐ ܡܛ̈ܐܬܐ
ܘܫܠܝ̈ܬܐ ܦ̈ܫܝܩܝܢ. ܘܐܝ̈ܬܝܐ ܙܟܘ̈ܬܐ ܘܠܐ ܡܛܝ̈ܒܬܐ ܡܬܦܪܥܝܢ. ܘܐܝ̈ܬܝܐ ܐܚܪܢ
ܡܛܝ̈ܒܬܐ ܒܟܠ ܚܕܐ ܙܟܘ̈ܬܐܡܛܝܒܝܢ ܘܐܬܦܪܥ ܕܦܫܩܝܢ. ܘܐܝ̈ܬܝܐܡܫܬܡܠܝܢ ܦܠܐ
ܘܫܠܡܝܢ ܘܚܕܝ̈ܢ ܡܛܝܒܝܢ܀

4. ܘܡܫܬܥܠܝܢ ܘܠܐ ܡܬܚܫܒܝܢ ܒܗܘܢ ܒܠܐ ܚܕܐ ܦܢܝܬܐ ܒܦܘܡ
ܘܡܛܝܒܝܢ. ܘܡܫܒܚܝܢ ܕܟܠ ܗܢܐ ܒܝܬ ܘܡܫܬܠܡܝܢ.* ܗܝܕܝܢ ܒܗܠ ܟܠܗܘܢ
ܡܬܚܫܒܝܢ ܕܟܠ ܒܢ̈ܝܐ ܕܒܚܒܠܐ ܐܘܪܚܐ ܒܢ̈ܝܢ ܘܢܒܥܘܢ ܒܗܘܢ ܢܦܫܐ ܡܫܡܫܢܐ
ܐܬܡܫܚܘ. ܡܚܝܐ ܬܚܘܬܐ ܠܟܠܗܘܢ ܦܪܫܐ ܒܢܩܦܘ ܒܟܠ ܐܢܘܫܐ. ܘܐܫܬܒܩ
ܕܡܫܝܢ ܒܟܠ ܡܫܝܚܘܬܐ. ܘܢܦܫܟܠ ܠܚܡܐ ܘܒܠܒܐ ܠܟܠܗܘܢ ܐܦܪܝ ܠܝ.
ܘܒܗܘܢ ܢܡܫܚ ܕܐܪܐ ܘܚܒܠܐ ܠܟܠܗܘܢ ܘܐܬܚܫܘܢ ܒܫܡܝ. ܘܒܗ ܡܢ ܒܗ
ܠܬܚܘܬܐ ܘܡܢܗ ܒܟܠ ܬܚܘܬܐ ܐܬܡܫܚ܆ ܘܡܫܠܡ ܦܘܡܐ ܒܗܘܢ ܘܒܗ
ܦܫܡܫܝܢ ܠܐܬܟܠ ܠܝ. ܐܦ ܐܫܬܡܥ ܘܒܟܠܝ ܐܝܟ ܕܐܬܐ ܠܡܫܬܡܠܐ ܐܦ ܠܐ
ܦܘܫ. ܘܡܫܘܚܐ ܘܠܐ ܡܟܠܐ ܢܦܩ ܠܟܠܡܫܬܐ ܚܕܬܐ ܦܘܚܠ ܬܚܘܬܐ
ܘܡܫܡܠܝܢ ܡܫܘܚܬܐ ܕܡܫܚܬܐ ܠܝ ܕܡܫܬܦܪܥ ܠܟܠܡܫܬܡܠܝܢ܀

5. *Explanation of the number of Prayers*: All the children of the Holy Church, (whether) bishops, priests, deacons or lay people think that the prayers of a day are seven. (But) they are not aware that they pray ten times and do not understand what they heard the divine Prophet David saying: "Seven times a day I praise you for your righteous ordinances (Ps. 119:164)". Because those of old who were guided under the ancient Law gave praise, that is prayed seven (times) a day, the number seven is being acclaimed (*mqallas*) among them [p. 4] having adopted this number seven from God's creations: in the holy scriptures they saw that there are seven heavens and the moving stars are 7. The whole number of the temporal world is 7000 'days' (i.e. years). One week is seven days. Moses lighted seven lamps on the lamp stand. Prophet Daniel prophesied on seven weeks. Thus the former (fathers) acknowledged (the significance) of the number seven. Formerly, there were Christians who saw that there are seven open doors in the head of a man through which the worldly senses[3] enter. (Therefore) they arranged seven prayers that each one of the (prayers) shall cleanse one door each. They acted (thus) reckoning that the external senses of a person consist of this number, forgetting the senses of touch, having (only) four (senses).

But Christians counted ten senses, external and internal. External: Vision, hearing, smell, taste, touch. Internal: rational mind (*hawno*), knowledge (*'ida'to*), understanding (*suklo*), intellect (*tar'itho*) and mind (*mad'o*). Thus, they have arranged ten prayers (corresponding) to the number of senses.

---

[3] Correct *gdš* to *rgš*.

5. ܢܘܗܪܐ ܡܛܠ ܡܫܝܚܐ ܕܙܟܘܬܐ:

ܒܗܘܢ ܒܢ̈ܝ ܕܝܪܐ ܡܠܒ̈ܫܝ ܐܣܟܝܡܐ ܘܒܢ̈ܬܐ ܘܡܫܡܫ̈ܢܐ ܘܟܠܟܗ̈ܢܐ ܫܒܚܝܢ ܕܙܟܘܬܐ ܗܟܢ ܐܬܝܢ ܒܝܘܡܐ ܚܕܐ. ܘܠܐ ܡܙܕܗܪܝܢ ܕܒܫܒ̈ܬܐ ܡܙܠܝܢ ܘܠܐ ܢܓܕܝܢ ܒ ܫܡܫܘ ܡܢ ܢܦܠܐ ܠܠܝܐ ܕܗܘ ܕܐܡܪ: ܫܒܥ ܒܝܘܡܐ ܫܒܚܬܟ ܥܠ ܕܝ̈ܢܐ ܙܕܝܩܐ. ܡܛܠ ܕܡܬܩܢܐ ܕܐܬܐܡܪܘ ܒܢܡܘܣܐ ܠܟܡܐ ܚܕ ܒܝܘܡܐ ܡܫܡܫܝܢ ܐܘܒܠ ܡܙܠܝܢ. ܕܡܫܝܚܐ ܡܫܒܚܐ ܡܩܠܣܗ* ܠܟܐܢܘܢ ܕܡܢ ܒܬܫܡܫܬܗ ܘܐܠܗܐ ܢܚܬܘܢ ܠܗܘܢ ܡܫܝܚܐ ܡܫܒܚܐ. ܘܡܢ ܒܠܝܠܐ ܡܕܢ̈ܚܐ ܕܝܠܗ ܘܐܝܟ ܫܦܝܪܐ ܫܒ̈ܐ. ܘܡܫܡܫܢܐ ܠܛܝܒܐ ܝܝ̄ ܐܝܟ. ܘܡܫܝܚܐ ܕܒܠܝܠܝܐ ܙܕܝܩܐ ܡܫ̈ܒܚܐ ܠܠܫܢ̈ܐ ܐܝܟܢ̄ܐ ܢܩܝܠܐ. ܡܫܒܚܐ ܢܩܘܫܐ ܐܝܟܢܐ ܡܫܒܚܬܐ. ܘܡܫܒܚܐ ܡܬܪܓܡ ܐܝܟ ܕܗܘܐ ܗܘܐ ܡܫܡܫܐ ܟ̈ܡܢܐ ܡܫܒܚܬܐ. ܘܒܫܠܡܐ ܐܬܝܢ ܡܛܠ ܡܫܒܚܬܐ. ܟܕ ܗܘܝܐ ܡܕܡܐ ܡܢ ܒܝܘܡܐ ܡܫܒܚܝܢ. ܘܐܝܟܢܐ ܕܬܫܒܚܬܐ ܕܗܘܘ ܡܕܡܐ ܕܝܠܗ ܘܐܝܟ ܒܝܢܘ ܕܒܢܝܐ ܡܫܒܚܐ ܠܐܪܥܐ ܦܠܚܝܐ ܘܡܫܒܚܘܢ ܢܟܝܢ ܠܟܠܗܘܢ ܒܟܠܗܘܢ ܩܠܐ[4] ܠܡܫܡܫܢܐ. ܫܒܚܘ ܙܟܘܬܐ ܡܫܒܚ ܠܡܫܝܚܐ ܕܡܠܗܘܢ. ܘܡܢ ܚܕܐ ܙܟܘܬܐ ܡܕܡܐ ܠܟܝ ܠܐܪܥܐ. ܘܡܫܒܚ ܩܠܐ ܒܬܪܐ ܕܒܢܝܐ ܚܣܝܢ ܒܗܘܢ ܡܫܝܚܐ. ܘܠܐ ܢܝܚ ܠܩܠܐ ܕܩܠܬܐ. ܘܫܒܚ ܒܫܡܗܘܢ ܐܪܥܐ. ܘܒܢܝܫܐ ܫܡܥܘ ܒܫܡܝܐ ܩܠܐ ܒܬܪܐ ܕܩܘܩܠܐ. ܒܬܪܐ: ܚܕܐ. ܡܫܒܚܐ. ܦܘܡܐ. ܠܡܫܒܚܬܐ. ܩܠܬܐ. ܕܢܘܡܐ: ܢܘܪܐ. ܢܒܥܬܐ. ܫܘܒܚܐ. ܠܐܪܥܬܐ. ܡܕܒܪܐ. ܒܠܠ ܗܘܝܐ ܠܫܡܗ ܒܫܡܝ ܙܟܘܬܐ ܒܫܡܝܢ ܩܠܐ ܕܒܫܡܗ܀

4 Ms ܩܕܝܫܐ

6. Again from the divine Prophet David who says, "Sing a new song to the Lord [p. 5] because he has done wonders" (Ps. 98:1). Again, "Sing a new praise to the Lord in the church of the righteous" (Ps. 149:1). Again, "Sing a new praise to the Lord! His praise from the ends of the earth" (Is. 42:10), that is, to leave behind the former praise which was seven (times a day) and 'Sing new praise' that is, ten (times). Again the prophet David speaks of ten praises in one Psalm (i.e.) Ps. 150.[5]

"Praise the Lord in his sanctuary; praise him in his mighty firmament. Praise him for his mighty deeds. Praise him according to the manifold greatness. Praise him with the sound of the horn. Praise him with harps and citterns. Praise him with tambourines and timbrels. Praise him with sweet string (instruments). Praise him with clashing of cymbals. Praise him with sound and shouting. Let everything that breathes praise the Lord".

By these ten, the tenfold praises or ten prayers were innovated for the Church.

7. Again this number has been confirmed by God's creations, by the Holy fathers, Mar Jacob and Mar Dionysius, one of the judge of the Areopagus, who received the divine knowledge (concerning) the spiritual orders of heaven, who consist of ten ranks [p. 6] They are the choirs of the angels: Archangels, Principalities, Authorities, Thrones, Lordships, Hosts, Cherubim and Seraphim who are standing near.

Again the order of the Holy Church of the human beings has ten ranks. They are: Patriarchs, Maphrians, Metropolitans, bishops, priests, deacons, sub-deacons, Chanters, readers and lay people.

---

[5] Read *qn* for *q* (ms. 100; but it must be 150).

6. ܬܘܒ ܡܢ ܒܬܪ ܠܐܠܗܐ ܕܗܘ ܕܐܡܪ ܡܫܚܗ ܒܩܢܝܐ ܠܡܫܘܚܬܐ* ܚܕܐ܆
ܡܛܠܠ ܕܠܐܘܡܢܝܬܐ ܟܠܗ. ܘܬܘܒ ܡܫܚܗ ܒܩܢܝܐ ܠܡܫܘܚܬܐ ܚܕܐ. ܠܡܫܘܚܬܗ
ܟܒܪܬܐ ܕܪܘܢܐ. ܬܘܒ ܡܫܚܗ ܒܩܢܝܐ ܠܡܫܘܚܬܐ ܚܕܐ ܠܡܫܘܚܬܗ ܡܢ
ܣܘܦܗ ܕܐܪܥܐ. ܗ̄ ܡܫܘܚܘ ܠܡܫܘܚܬܐ ܦܬܝܚܬܐ ܕܐܝܟܢܐ ܡܫܚ.
ܘܠܡܫܘܚܬܐ ܚܕܐ ܡܫܚܗ ܕܐܝܟܢܐ ܟܡܐ. ܬܘܒ ܕܗܘ ܒܬܪ ܐܡܪ ܟܡ̈ܐ
ܠܡܫܚܬܐ ܚܕ ܡܬܡܫܚܐ ܕܩܡ ܡܫܚܗ ܒܩܢܝܐ ܒܡܫܘܚܬܗ. ܡܫܚܘܗܝ ܒܪܘܡܗ
ܘܒܦܬܝܗ. ܡܫܚܘܗܝ ܒܡܫܘܚܬܗ. ܡܫܚܘܗܝ ܒܥܘܡܩܗ ܕܐܪܥܐ. ܡܫܚܘܗܝ
ܒܟܠܐ ܕܡܪܢܐ. ܡܫܚܘܗܝ ܒܥܠܬܐ ܘܒܡܢܝܢܐ. ܡܫܚܘܗܝ ܒܦܠܓܘܬܐ ܘܒܪ̈ܟܢܐ.
ܡܫܚܘܗܝ ܒܡܢܝܢܐ ܣܘܓܐܐ. ܡܫܚܘܗܝ ܒܪ̈ܓܠܝ ܩܘܡܬܐ. ܡܫܚܘܗܝ ܒܟܠܐ
ܘܡܟܝܠܬܐ. ܘܦܠܐ ܢܡܘܣܐ ܠܡܟܣ ܠܩܢܝܐ. ܡܢ ܗܠܝܢ ܒܫܢܐ ܐܬܚܙܝܬ ܠܟܠܗ
ܟܡܐ ܠܡܫܘܚܬܐ ܐܘܪܟܗ ܟܡܐ ܦܬܝܗܐ❖
7. ܘܬܘܒ ܡܢ ܒܬܪܗ ܕܐܠܗܐ ܐܬܚܙܝ ܗܘܐ ܡܫܝܚܐ. ܠܐܬܪ̈ܝ ܐܪܒܥܬܐ ܩܕ̈ܝܫܐ
ܡܢܗ ܡܠܟܘܬ ܘܡܢܗ ܕܣܘܣܦܘܣ ܕܡܢ ܕ̈ܝܢܐ ܕܐܪܥܐ ܦܠܚܘܗ ܘܡܠܟܘ ܡܢ
ܚܕܬܐ ܠܐܠܗܐ ܕܠܐܡܬܐ ܕܢܘܚܐ ܕܒܫܡܝܐ ܟܡ̈ܐ ܡܫܘܚܬܐ ܐܝܟ.*ܡܡܫܚܝܢ
ܘܐܝܬܝܗܘܢ ܡܠܐܟ̈ܐ. ܪ̈ܝܫ ܡܠܐܟ̈ܐ. ܪ̈ܝܫܢܘܬܐ. ܫܘܠܛܢ̈ܐ. ܡܪ̈ܘܬܐ. ܟܘܪ̈ܣܘܬܐ. ܟܪ̈ܘܒܐ.
ܣܪ̈ܦܐ. ܡܠܐܟܝ ܪ̈ܘܚܐ.
ܬܘܒ ܛܟܣܐ ܕܒܬܪ ܩܕܡܝܬܐ ܘܐܪ̈ܟܢܐ. ܟܡ̈ܐ ܡܫܘܚܬܐ ܐܝܟ܇ ܘܐܝܬܝܗܘܢ.
ܦܛܪ̈ܝܪܟܐ. ܡܦܪ̈ܝܢܐ. ܡܝܛܪ̈ܘܦܘܠܝܛܐ. ܐܦܣܩܘܦ̈ܐ. ܩܫ̈ܝܫܐ. ܡܫܡ̈ܫܢܐ.
ܐܦܘܕܝܩܢ̈ܐ. ܦܣܠܛ̈ܐ. ܐܢܓܢܘܣܛ̈ܐ. ܥܠܡܝ̈ܐ.

Again in the venerable and Holy Gospel, our Lord gave ten beatitudes to the Holy Church. Though Mathew mentions (only) nine beatitudes, as he left out the tenth beatitude (Matt. 5:1–11). But in Luke, there is: "Blessed are those who weep, for they shall laugh" (Lk. 6:21). Every beatitude is said regarding one prayer, which we shall explain after this, if God wills.

8. Again it is said in the venerable and holy Gospel: "What king, going to encounter another king in war, will not sit down first and take counsel whether he is able with ten thousand to meet him who comes against him with twenty thousand? And if not, while the other is yet far away from him, he sends (an embassy) and seeks what is (needed) for peace" (Luke 14:31–32). And the king who has ten thousand (soldiers) [p. 7] that is, the man having ten senses of body and spirit. Five are bodily: vision, hearing, smell, taste (and) touch. And the five of the soul: reason (*hawno*), wisdom (*ḥekamtho*), conscience (*re'yono*), intellect (*tar'itho*) and mind (*mad'o*). And the king having twenty thousand is the world and its twenty desires.

Five of necessities: Food, drink, dress, house and sleep.

Five of actual existence: Buying, selling, sowing, planting and workmanship.

Five (others) are: Avarice, jealousy, greed, enmity and slander.

Five alien ones are: Murder, adultery, theft, falsehood, infidelity.

Because of these ten things, ten prayers a day are arranged in the Holy Church, that is, in the night and in the day. By their daily celebration, the ten senses of the soul and the body are cleansed and God the Creator of the senses and the One who sets the creation in order is glorified. To Him be glory forever.

ܬܘܒ ܐܘܩܠܝܕܝܣ ܦܝܠܣܘܦܐ ܘܚܟܝܡܐ. ܒܣܦܪ̈ܐ ܛܘ̈ܦܐ ܡܢܗ ܡܢܝ ܒܟܬܒܘܗܝ ܡܕܝܢܬܐ.
ܐܦ ܡܢܗ ܒܗܘ ܐܡܪ ܛܘ̈ܦܐ ܐܠܐ ܛܘܦܐ ܒܡܢܝܢܐ ܡܬܡܢܐ ܠܗܘܢܐ ܕܐܝܬܘ̄
ܛܘܦܣܘܗܝ ܗܘܝ ܕܟܠܗ ܐܝܬܘܗܝ ܗܘ ܡܛܠ ܕܐܝܬܝܗܘܢ. ܕܟܠ ܛܘܦܐ ܐܡܪ
ܡܛܠ ܚܕܐ ܙܒܢܬܐ ܕܐܝܬܝܗܝܢ ܕܡܫܡܫ ܐܢܘܢ. ܒܬܪ ܗܠܝܢ ܕܐܟܘܬܐ ܕܙܒܢܐ܀
8. ܘܬܘܒ ܐܡܪ ܠܐܘܩܠܝܕܝܣ ܦܝܠܣܘܦܐ ܐܘ ܡܕܝܢܐ. ܐܘ ܡ̈ܠܘܗܝ ܡܟܠܟܐ ܕܡܢ ܐܪܐܠ
ܠܡܪܩܘܣ ܒܡ ܡܟܠܟܐ ܐܡܪܢܐ ܒܡܪܟܐ ܠܐ ܢܗܘܐ ܡܕܝܢܬܐ ܡܬܚܫܒ ܕܐܢ ܐܝܬܘ̄
ܘܡܕܐ ܒܡܡ̈ܪܐ ܠܠܫܢܐ ܠܡܬܪܓܡ ܠܗܘ ܕܒܡ ܒܡ̈ܪܝܢ ܠܠܫܢܐ ܐܬܐ ܒܟܠܗܘܢ:
ܘܐܢܝ ܠܐ. ܒܝ ܒܕܡܠܐ ܢܣܒ ܡܢܗ ܐܝܬܘ̄: ܘܐܢ ܠܐ ܡܕܐ : ܡܢܝܢ ܘܡܣܡܣ
ܗܠܝܢ ܕܟܠܐ ܚܝܠ. ܘܡܟܠܟܐ ܕܐܝܬ ܒܡܢܗ ܒܡ̈ܪܐ ܠܠܫܢܐ* ܗܘܢܘ ܒܪܢܫܐ ܕܐܝܬ
ܠܗ ܒܡ̈ܪܐ ܩܝܣܐ ܦܓܪܢܝܐ ܘܢܦܫܢܝܐ. ܚܡܫܐ ܦܓܪ̈ܢܝܐ: ܚܙܘܐ. ܫܡܥܐ. ܡܘܚܐ.
ܛܥܡܬܐ. ܓܫܬܐ. ܘܚܡܫܐ ܢܦܫ̈ܢܝܐ: ܗܘܢܐ. ܡܚܫܒܬܐ. ܪܥܝܢܐ. ܬܪܥܝܬܐ.
ܡܕܥܐ. ܘܡܟܠܟܐ ܕܐܝܬ ܒܡܢܗ ܒܡ̈ܪܝܢ ܠܠܫܢܐ ܗܘܢܘ ܒܟܠܡܐ. ܘܒܡ̈ܪܝܢ
ܩ̈ܪܝܬܗ ܘܐܝܬܝܗܝܢ.

ܚܡܫ ܐܢܢܩ̈ܝܬܐ: ܡܐܟܠܐ. ܡܫܬܝܐ. ܠܒܘܫܐ. ܒܝܬܐ. ܫܢܬܐ.
ܚܡܫ ܡܪ̈ܓܫܢܝܬܐ ܐܝܬܝܗܝܢ : ܚܙܝܐ ܘܫܡܥܐ. ܪܝܚܐ. ܛܥܡܐ. ܓܫܘܫܘܬܐ.
ܘܚܡܫ ܐܝܬܝܗܝܢ ܡ̈ܢܘܬܐ. ܫܘܫܠܐ. ܚܠܘܒܘܬܐ. ܦ̈ܠܛܬܐ. ܡܐܟܠܬܐ.
ܘܚܡܫ ܢܦܫ̈ܢܝܬܐ ܐܝܬܝܗܝܢ. ܡܛܠ. ܐܘܣܝܐ. ܚܝܘܬܐ. ܕܝܠܝܘܬܐ. ܦܘܪܫܐ.

ܡܛܠ ܗܠܝܢ ܒܡ̈ܪܘܬܐ ܐܬܩܪܝ ܒܡ̈ܪ ܙܒ̈ܢܬܐ ܒܟܬܒܬܐ ܡܕܝܢܬܐ ܒܡܢ ܡ̈ܘܫܐ
ܐܘܟܝܬ ܒܠܫܢܐ ܐܘܩܠܝܕܝܣ. ܗܘܡܟܠ ܡ̈ܘܫܐ ܕܒܗܘܢ ܢܬܝܕܥ ܒܡ̈ܪܐ ܩ̈ܪܝܐ
ܢܦܫܐ ܘܦܓܪܢܝܐ. ܘܒܗܘܢ ܢܬܟܪܒ ܠܐܠܗܐ ܒܪܘܫܐ ܕܩ̈ܪܝܐ ܘܡܬܛܟܣܢܐ ܕܒܪ̈ܝܬܐ
ܕܠܗ ܫܘܒܚܐ ܠܥܠܡܝܢ܀

9. *Order of the ten prayers of the night and the day, of a Sunday.*

Regulation of the prayers ordained by the holy fathers is as follows [**8**]: From sunset to morning, (there are) five prayers: *Sutoro* and the four nocturns (*'edone*) of the night. And from the rising of the sun to evening (*Ramso*) (there are) five prayers: *Sapro*, third hour, Midday, which is the Sixth hour, and the Ninth hour, and *Ramsho.*[6] Night and day are divided into four parts. Each part (consists of) six hours. From (one) six to (another) six, common prayer is celebrated. In the evening (themes are) common and midnight (also) common; [in the morning common and (also) in the midday common].[7]

(On) *Qurbono,* that is the prayer of midday.[8] And if by chance, *qurbono* is not offered, common prayer shall be celebrated at midday. And on the week days at the hour of evening and morning *'enyono* is common; *sedro* is common; and *qole* are (also) common.

Then suitable *sedro* of the day and *qolo* that follows it and the *bo'utho* in the tone that is assigned for the Sunday, so that the tone of that day is made distinct in the night, and in the day time (*'imomo*), at *Ramsho, Sapro* and *Sutoro.* Again it's *qolo* with *bo'utho* or *takshaphto* sung in the tone of the day.

If someone sings on the ordinary week days, the common (prayers) should be said without tone. This is because of ignorance: he is rebuked the prayers of the night, third hour and sixth [**9**] and ninth, because they are sung in the tone of the day. Thus all prayers shall be assigned the tone of the day. In *Ramsho* and in *Sapro* of the days of the week, the priest should not read the *sedro* of penitence which is not common.

---

[6] But according to custom, a day begins with the evening.

[7] Written in the right margin.

[8] It is interesting to note that midday prayer is called *Qurbono* (some words are apparently missing here).

9. ܛܘܒܢܐ ܕܒܗܢ ܙܒܢ̈ܬܐ ܘܒܠܠܝܐ ܘܒܐܝܡܡܐ ܕܡܕܒܪܐ:
ܐܢܫܐ ܕܒܙܒܢ̈ܬܐ ܕܐܬܛܫܝܘ ܡܢ ܐܒܗ̈ܬܐ ܩܕܝܫ̈ܐ ܗܘܝܢ* ܐܝܠܝܢ. ܡܢ ܡܕܝܢ̈ܬܐ
ܥܡܡܐ ܠܒܪܐ ܢܦܩܘ ܙܒܢ̈ܬܐ: ܡܫܪܐ ܘܐܘܪܚܐ ܕܒܪ̈ܝܐ ܕܠܗܠ. ܘܡܢ ܡܕܝܢ̈ܬܐ
ܥܡܡܐ ܠܡܕܒܪܐ ܢܦܩܘ ܙܒܢ̈ܬܐ: ܕܒܪܐ. ܕܐܬܟܠܡܢܝܢ. ܕܦܠܓܘܗ̇ ܕܡܫܐ: ܕܡܠܐ
ܐܠܗܐ. ܕܐܡܝܢ ܡܢܝܢ. ܕܢܡܘܣܐ. ܐܬܦܠܓܘܗ̇ ܠܟܠܐ ܘܐܡܡܘܬܐ ܠܐܪܒܥ ܡܢ̈ܘܬܐ. ܟܠ
ܡܢܬܐ ܠܗ ܡܢܐ. ܘܡܢ ܗܠܝܢ ܠܗܝܢ ܙܒܢ̈ܬܐ ܥܘܢܝܬܐ ܡܫܠܡܢܝܬܐ. ܒܕܡܘܬܐ
ܥܘܢܝܬܐ ܘܒܦܠܓܘܗ̇ ܕܟܠܐ ܥܘܢܝܬܐ. ܘܒܪ̈ܐ ܥܘܢܝܬܐ ܘܒܦܠܓܘܗ̇ ܕܡܘܬܐ
ܥܘܢܝܬܐ.

ܘܡܘܪܒܐ ܗܘܘ ܙܒܢܝܗ ܕܦܠܓܘܗ̇ ܕܡܘܬܐ. ܘܐܦ ܐܢܫ ܘܠܐ ܢܛܪܝܢ ܡܘܪܒܐ
ܙܒܢܐ ܥܘܢܝܬܐ ܠܡܫܡܠܝܘ ܒܦܠܓܘܗ̇ ܕܡܘܬܐ. ܘܒܩܝܡܬܐ ܕܡܟܠܐ ܒܟܪܝܐ
ܕܡܘܬܐ ܘܕܒܪܐ ܡܢܡܢܗ ܒܢܝܐ ܥܘܢܝܐ. ܡܪܬܐ ܥܘܢܝܐ ܘܟܠܐ ܥܘܢܝܐ.

ܘܡܬܪܡ ܡܪܬܐ ܕܒܢܝܢ ܒܡܘܬܐ ܘܟܠܐ ܕܢܦܩ ܠܗ ܘܒܟܠܐ ܒܡܢܝܬܐ ܕܢܦܫܐ
ܒܢܝܢ ܒܟܬܒܐ ܕܐܬܦܪܫ ܡܢܝܢܗ ܕܗܘ ܡܘܬܐ ܒܟܠܐ ܘܒܐܝܡܡܐ ܘܒܪܝܬܐ
ܘܒܪܐ. ܘܡܫܬܪܐ. ܠܐܘܒ ܟܠܐ ܕܝܠܗ ܒܡ ܒܟܘܬܐ ܐܘ ܠܡܫܠܡܬܐ ܒܡܢܝܬܐ ܕܝܠܗ
ܕܡܘܬܐ ܢܫܬܡܠܐ.

ܘܐܦ ܐܝܟ ܕܐܡܪ ܕܩܪܝܬܐ ܡܫܝܚܝܬܐ ܕܡܠܬܐ: ܡܫܝܚܝܐ ܗܘܝܢ ܕܢܛܪ ܘܠܐ ܡܢܝܬܐ.
ܗܘܐ ܡܢ ܠܐ ܢܒܥܬܐ ܐܬܡܠܝ. ܘܡܫܡܫ ܠܗ ܙܒܢ̈ܬܐ ܕܟܠܐ ܘܐܬܟܠܡ ܡܢܝܢ
ܘܕܡܢܝܢ* ܘܐܬܦܠܓ ܡܬܠܠ ܕܒܡܢܝܬܐ ܕܡܘܬܐ ܡܫܬܡܪܝܢ. ܒܟܠ ܗܘܝܢ ܙܒܢ
ܕܒܟܠܗܘܢ ܙܒܢ̈ܬܐ ܡܢܝܢܗ ܕܡܘܬܐ ܐܬܦܪܫ.

This is done by those who are ignorant before God. But first, common sedro, common *qole*, and after that the suitable *sedro*, that is, first they take refuge in the Theotokos and the holy martyrs, for they have confidence before God. Then they supplicate repentance for the sinners and absolution for the departed. There are ignorant clergy who also do not recite the common *sedro* in the *Ramsho* and in *Sapro* of the week days, but (say) a single *sedro* appropriate for the day, saying that it is sufficient. They do not know that it is laxity and presumption before God. Consequently their prayer is not accepted. Rather, it brings down wrath from heaven upon those who pray with laxity, and if they do not complete it in full, they are rebuked the common *qole* of the Breviary (*shḥimo*), which are common: that there are stanzas (*bote*) of the Theotokos, martyrs, repentance and the departed. How can they sing the common *qole* without the common s*edro*? This is an error!

Again they should understand from the prayers of *Lilyo*: in the first nocturn (*'edono*), they make intercession of the Theotokos [**10**] and in the second *'edono*, they take refuge in the martyrs, and in the third nocturn is for repentance or for the departed (depending on) the day. And the fourth nocturn in summary is again common. According to the Deuteronomy of Moses, again the Lord will make his right hand greater and will hear the prayers that are offered to Him.

10. *Confirmation of the prayers of the ordinary days of a week*:

Monday *Ramsho 'enyono* is common; *sedro*, common; two (sets of) *qole* of the Breviary (*shḥimo*) are common. Again *quqliun* and *sedro* (are) of repentance, or of the Evening; also the *qolo* and *bo'utho* are of repentance. And in *Sutoro*: *sedro* of repentance; *qolo* and *bo'utho* or supplication (*takshepto*) are of repentance. And in *Lilyo*, first nocturn (*'edono*) is for the Theotokos and second nocturn (*'edono*) for the holy martyrs, and the third nocturn for repentance and the fourth nocturn is common. And after their completion, they commemorate the saint of the (local) church.

ܘܠܐ ܙܘܥ ܕܒܢ̈ܝܐ ܒܪܡܫܐ ܐܘ ܒܨܦܪܐ ܕܢ̈ܡܫܬܐ ܘܡܫܟܬܐ ܢܫܡܫܘܢ ܚܙܘܐ ܕܐܝܬܘܬܐ
ܘܠܐ ܓܘܢܐ. ܗܕܐ ܡܢ ܠܐ ܡܕܟܝܐ ܐܝܟܢܘ ܩܕܡ ܐܠܗܐ. ܐܠܐ ܡܕܡܝܢ ܚܙܘܐ ܓܘܢܐ
ܘܟܠ ܓܘ̈ܢܐ ܘܡܬܪܨ ܚܙܘܐ ܕܒܣܡ ܐܘܟܡܐ ܡܕܡܟ ܡܬܓܘܫܢ ܒܡܟܕܐ
ܐܠܗܐ ܘܒܡܕܪܐ ܡܕܝܢܐ ܕܐܗܘܐ ܒܗܘܢ ܦܪܘܫܘܬܐ ܩܕܡ ܐܠܗܐ. ܘܡܬܪܨ ܢܒܗܘܢ
ܐܝܬܘܬܐ ܒܡܠܟܬܐ ܘܣܘܟܠܐ ܒܟܝܢܐ. ܕܐܝܟ ܒܢ̈ܝܐ ܠܐ ܡܕܒܪ ܒܪܡܫܐ ܘܒܨܦܪܐ
ܕܡܬܐ ܚܙܘܐ ܓܘܢܐ ܒܗ ܡܫܡܫܢ ܐܠܐ ܡܢ ܚܙܘܐ ܕܒܣܡ ܒܗܘܡܐ. ܘܦܫܫ
ܐܡܪܢ ܘܠܐ ܡܕܡܢ ܕܪܘܫܘܬܐ ܘܡܬܪ̈ܡܝܢܘܬܐ ܐܝܟܢܘ ܩܕܡ ܐܠܗܐ. ܘܒܗܘܢ ܕܠܐ
ܡܬܡܟܠܐ ܕܒܗܝܘܢ. ܐܠܐ ܪܡܙܐ ܡ̈ܢܬܐ ܡܢ ܫܡܝܐ ܥܠ ܡܪ̈ܟܒܬܐ ܕܪܘܫܘܬܐ.
ܘܐܢ ܠܐ ܢܣܬܟܠܘܢ ܒܗܕܐ ܟܠ ܓܘ̈ܢܐ ܕܡܢܝܢܐ ܡܫܡܫܢ ܒܗܘܢ ܕܓܘ̈ܢܝܐ ܐܝܟܢ.
ܕܐܝܟ ܒܗܘܢ ܟܠܗ ܒܡܕܝܢܬܐ ܐܠܗܐ ܘܒܡܕܪܐ ܘܒܐܝܬܘܬܐ ܘܒܟܝܢܐ. ܐܡܪ
ܐܡܪܢ ܟܠ ܓܘ̈ܢܐ ܘܠܐ ܚܙܘܐ ܓܘܢܐ. ܗܕܐ ܕܟܝܘܬܐ ܐܝܟܢܘ.
ܘܐܘܟ ܡܢ ܕܒܢ̈ܬܐ ܕܟܠܢܐ ܢܫܬܡܥܘܢ ܕܒܕܝܢܐ ܡܕܡܝܐ ܡܫܬܡܫܢ ܒܡܟܕܐ
ܐܠܗܐ. ܘܒܕܝܢܐ* ܬܪܝܢܐ ܡܬܓܘܫܢ ܒܡܕܪܐ ܘܒܕܝܢܐ ܬܠܝܬܝܐ ܒܗ ܒܗܘܡܐ
ܒܐܝܬܘܬܐ ܐܘ ܒܟܝܢܐ. ܘܒܕܝܢܐ ܪܒܝܥܝܐ ܒܫܡܝܐ ܘܐܝܣܘܬܐ ܓܘܢܝܢ ܐܝܟܘ ܐܝܟ
ܬܢܢ ܢܗܘܬܐ ܡܘܡܝܐ. ܕܢܘܫܦ ܡܪܝܐ ܬ݂ܢܝܐ ܕܡܫܝܚܐ ܘܡܫܟܢ ܕܒܢ̈ܬܐ ܕܡܬܡܪ̈ܢܝܢ
ܒܗ܀

10. ܫܘܪܪܐ ܕܕܒܢܬܐ ܒܩܘܫܬܐ ܡܬܪܕܝܢܐ ܕܡܟܬܐ:
ܒܪܡܫܐ ܕܬܪܝܢ ܒܡܟܐ ܒܣܢܐ ܓܘܢܐ. ܘܚܙܘܐ ܓܘܢܐ. ܟܠ ܬܪܝܢ ܡܬܪܕܝܢܐ
ܓܘ̈ܢܐ ܘܐܘܟ ܡܡܟܠܗܘܢ ܘܚܙܘܐ ܒܐܝܬܘܬܐ ܐܘ ܒܪܡܫܐ. ܘܟܠ ܘܒܗܘܬܐ
ܒܐܝܬܘܬܐ. ܘܒܡܘܬܪܐ ܚܙܘܐ ܕܐܝܬܘܬܐ ܘܟܠ ܘܒܗܘܬܐ ܐܘ ܬܡܝܡܬܐ ܕܐܝܬܘܬܐ.
ܘܟܠܟܠܐ ܕܝܢܐ ܡܕܡܝܐ ܒܡܟܕܐ ܐܠܗܐ ܘܒܕܝܢܐ ܬܪܝܢܐ ܒܡܕܪܐ ܡܕܝܢܐ. ܘܒܕܝܢܐ
ܬܠܝܬܝܐ ܒܐܝܬܘܬܐ. ܘܒܕܝܢܐ ܪܒܝܥܝܐ ܒܓܘܢܐ. ܘܟܠܪ ܫܘܡܠܝܐ ܡܬܒܗܘܢ
ܒܡܕܝܢܐ ܕܐܝܟ ܒܕܝܢܐ.

And on [Monday] *Sapro*: *'enyono* and *sedro* are common. *Qole* (are) common; and again *quqliun* and *sedro* (are) of repentance or of morning (*saphro*): *qolo, bo'utho* that follow the *sedro* (are common). And in the third hour, *Sedro* [is] for repentance and (also) *qolo* and *bo'utho*.

At the sixth hour of *Qurobo, sedro, qolo* and *bo'utho* are common. At the ninth hour, the *sedro* is for the departed (as well as) *qolo* and the *bo'utho* that follow.

[**11**] Tuesday: *Ramsho, Lilyo, Sapro* and the whole day is as on the previous Monday. Wednesday *Ramsho*: *'enyono, sedro, qolo* and *bo'utho* are common. *Sutoro* is of repentance. And in *Lilyo*, first nocturn (*'edono*) is for Theotokos, second for the martyrs, third for the departed and the fourth is general. After their completion, they commemorate the saint (according to) all the days of the year.

In *Sapro*: *'enyono, sedro* are common and the *qolo* and then the *quqliun* is for the Theotokos. The *qolo* and *Bo'utho* are common. Third hour is for the Theotokos; *sedro, qolo* and *bo'utho* are common. Sixth hour *qurbono* is celebrated or common [prayers are said]. Ninth hour is always for the departed.

Thursday *Ramsho*: *'enyono* and *sedro* are common, also (a sedro) of repentance. *Sutoro* is as usual. In *Lilyo*, the first nocturn (*'edono*) is for the Theotokos, the second for the Apostles; the third for repentance and the fourth common and the final *bo'utho* for the apostles. And *Sapro* as well as the rest of the day, is as on Monday and Tuesday.

Friday *Ramsho*: *'enyono* and *sedro* are common. Again *quqliun* and *Sedro* for the martyrs, *qolo* and *bo'utho* common [**12**] and *Sutoro* as usual.

ܘܡܪ̈ܥܐ ܒܢܫܐ ܘܥܒܕܐ ܒܥܝܪܐ. ܘܩܠܐ ܒܩܘܫܐ. ܘܐܘܒ ܣܘܣܟܘܢ ܘܥܒܕܐ
ܕܐܝܡܘܬܐ ܐܘ ܕܪ̈ܥܐ. ܘܡܠܐ ܘܡܘܬܐ ܕܢܦܩ ܠܥܒܕܐ. ܘܟܠܠܟ ܫ̈ܢܝܢ ܥܒܕܐ
ܠܐܝܡܘܬܐ ܘܡܠܐ ܘܡܘܬܐ.
ܘܦ̈ܠܓܐ ܫܢܝܢ ܕܡܘܪܒܐ ܐܘ ܥܒܕܐ ܒܥܝܪܐ ܘܡܠܐ ܘܡܘܬܐ. ܘܟܠܡܫ ܫܢܝܢ ܥܒܕܐ
ܠܢܫ̈ܕܐ ܘܡܠܐ ܘܡܘܬܐ ܕܢܦܩ ܠܗܘ܀*
ܒܪܡܫܐ ܕܐܝܠܠܐ ܒܡܫܐ. ܒܡ ܠܠܝܐ ܘܪ̈ܥܐ ܘܦܠܓܗ ܢ̈ܘܫܐ ܐܝܟ ܡܘܫܐ ܕܐܪܥ
ܒܡܫܐ ܐܟܠܐ̄ ܗܘ ܕܒܒܪ. ܪܡܫܐ ܕܐܪܒܥܐ ܒܡܫܐ ܒܢܫܐ ܘܥܒܕܐ ܘܡܠܐ ܘܡܘܬܐ
ܒܥܝܪܐ. ܘܢܗܘܪܐ ܠܐܝܡܘܬܐ ܘܟܠܠܝܐ ܒܕܝܐ ܡܕܝܢܐ ܠܡܠܟܐ ܠܠܗܐ. ܘܐܘܪܚܐ
ܠܢܫ̈ܕܐ. ܘܐܠܟܠܝܐ ܠܢܫ̈ܕܐ ܘܪܟܡܝܐ ܠܒܥܝܪܐ. ܘܟܠܪ ܡܘܫܟܝܐ ܡܠܟܘܬܝܢ
ܠܡܕܝܢܬܐ܆ ܦܠܓܘܢ ܢ̈ܘܫܐ ܚܝܠܐ.
ܘܡܪ̈ܥܐ ܒܢܫܐ ܘܥܒܕܐ ܒܥܝܪܐ ܘܩܠܐ ܘܟܠܪܘܢ ܡܘܫܟܝܢ ܠܡܠܟܐ ܠܠܗܐ. ܘܡܠܐ
ܘܡܘܬܐ ܒܥܝܪܬܐ. ܘܟܠܠܟ ܫܢܝܢ ܠܡܠܟܐ ܠܠܗܐ ܥܒܕܐ ܘܡܠܐ ܘܡܘܬܐ
ܒܥܝܪܬܐ. ܘܦܠܓܗ ܫܢܝܢ ܡܘܪܒܐ ܢܦܠܡܠܐ ܐܘ ܒܥܝܪܐ ܘܟܠܡܫ ܫܢܝܢ
ܠܢܫ̈ܕܐ ܦܠܓܘܢ ܢ̈ܘܫܐ ܒܠܡܫܐ܀
ܪܡܫܐ ܕܚܡܫܐ ܒܡܫܐ. ܒܢܫܐ ܘܥܒܕܐ ܒܥܝܪܐ ܘܐܘܒ ܕܐܝܡܘܬܐ. ܘܡܫܬܐܐ ܐܝܟ
ܒܢܝܐ. ܘܟܠܠܝܐ܆ ܒܕܝܐ ܡܕܝܢܐ ܠܡܠܟܐ ܠܠܗܐ. ܬܐܘܪܚܐ ܠܡܠܟܘܬܐ.ܘܐܟܠܝܬܐ
ܠܐܝܡܘܬܐ. ܘܪܟܡܝܐ ܒܥܝܬܐ ܘܡܘܬܐ ܐܣܢܝܬܐ ܠܡܠܟܘܬܐ. ܘܡܪ̈ܥܐ ܘܡܘܟܠܡ
ܢ̈ܘܫܐ ܐܝܟ ܡܘܫܐ ܕܐܪܥ ܘܐܟܠܬܐ܀
ܪܡܫܐ ܕܒܪܘܟܬܐ. ܒܢܫܐ ܘܥܒܕܐ ܒܥܝܪܐ. ܘܐܘܒ ܣܘܣܟܘܢ ܘܥܒܕܐ ܠܥܒ̈ܕܐ
ܘܡܠܐ ܘܡܘܬܐ ܒܥܝܪܬܐ.* ܘܡܫܬܐܐ ܐܝܟ ܒܢܝܐ.

And Lilyo during summer (*qaiṭo*) from the feast of Resurrection to *Qudosh 'Edtho,*[9] the first nocturn (*'edono*) is for the Cross, (as well as) *Sedro, qolo* and *bo'utho.* And the second (nocturn) for the martyrs; third for the departed, and the fourth is common. After the fourth (nocturn), *quqliun* and *sedro* are for the Theotokos with common *qolo* and *bo'utho.*

In *Sapro*: *'enyono* is of the cross; sedro is common; *qole, quqliun* are of the cross; *sedro, qolo* and *bo'utho* are also of the cross. Third hour has its own *sedro* and *qolo* and *bo'utho* are for the cross. Sixth for the *qurbono*; ninth hour for the departed as usual.

From *Qudosh 'edtho* to the [Great] Lent every Sunday has its own order.

First, *Qudosh 'edtho*: In *Ramsho* of the *Qudosh 'edtho,* they say *'enyono, sedro, qolo, hulolo* and the Gospel. Again *quqliun* is for the departed, *sedro, qolo* and *bo'utho* for the *Qudosh 'edto*; and *Sutoro* as usual. In *Lilyo,* first nocturn for the *Qudosh 'edto.* For the next nocturn (again) for *Qudosh 'edto*; the third for the departed as usual and the fourth is common as usual, and the rest (also) as usual. *Sapro* for *Qudosh 'edto.* Third hour for *Qudosh 'edto,* and the rest of the day as usual.

In Friday *Ramsho*: *'enyono, Sedro* and *qolo* are common; **[13]** *quqliun, sedro* and *qolo* for the martyrs, and *bo'utho* is common. *Sutoro* as usual. And in *Lilyo*: first nocturn, for Theotokos, the second for the martyrs, the third for the departed and the fourth is common and also (*tub*) for the saint of the (local) church.

---

[9] Lit: 'Sanctification of the Church'. *Qudosh 'Edtho* is the first Sunday of the Syrian Orthodox liturgical year. 30/31st October, if falls on a Sunday. Otherwise the first Sunday of November. The second Sunday is called *Hudosh 'Edtho*: 'Dedication or Renewal of the Church'.

ܘܟܠܗܝܢ ܟܘ̈ܟܒܐ ܡܢ ܓܠܘܐ ܘܡܢܥܠܬܐ ܠܦܘܬ ܒܝܬܐ. ܒܝܬܐ ܩܕܡܝܐ ܠܙܟܘܬܐ
ܗܕܪܐ ܘܗܠܐ ܘܡܘܬܐ. ܘܐܘܪܚܐ ܠܫܘ̈ܩܐ ܘܐܠܗ̈ܝܬܐ ܠܟܢ̈ܫܐ ܘܙܒܢܐ ܠܢܘܚܐ.
ܘܟܠܙ ܙܒܢܐ ܡܡܠܟܘܗܝ ܘܗܕܪܐ ܠܡܠܟܐ ܠܐܠܗܐ: ܟܡ ܡܠܐ ܘܡܘܬܐ ܠܢܘܚܐ.
ܘܪܦܙܐ ܚܝܐ ܘܙܟܘܬܐ ܘܗܕܪܐ ܠܢܘܚܐ ܟܡ ܩܠܐ ܘܡܡܠܟܘܗܝ ܘܙܟܘܬܐ ܘܗܕܪܐ
ܘܗܠܐ ܘܡܘܬܐ ܠܙܟܘܬܐ. ܐܠܗܐ ܫܢܝܢ ܘܡܟܝܠܐ ܗܕܪܐ ܘܗܠܐ ܘܡܘܬܐ ܠܙܟܘܬܐ.
ܗܠܐ ܫܢܝܢ ܠܡܘܙܒܠܐ ܘܐܠܗܐ ܫܢܝܢ ܠܟܢ̈ܫܐ ܐܝܟ ܟܢܫܐ.
ܘܡܢ ܡܘܕܥ ܒܝܬܐ ܒܕܡܐ ܠܪܘܡܐ ܦܠܐ ܣܝܟܡܬܐ ܠܫܡܫܐ ܘܡܟܝܠܐ ܐܝܟ ܟܘ.
ܩܕܡܝܐ ܡܘܕܥ ܒܝܬܐ. ܒܙܡܢܐ ܠܦܘܬ ܒܝܬܐ ܐܡܙܝܢ ܚܝܢܐ ܘܗܕܪܐ ܘܗܠܐ
ܘܡܘܠܠܐ ܘܐܘܢܟܘܗܝ. ܘܐܘܟ ܡܡܠܟܘܗܝ ܠܟܢܫܐ. ܘܗܕܪܐ ܘܗܠܐ ܘܡܘܬܐ
ܠܦܘܬ ܒܝܬܐ ܘܗܘܠܐܐ ܐܝܟ ܟܢܫܐ. ܘܟܠܗܝܢ ܒܝܬܐ ܩܕܡܝܐ ܠܦܘܬ ܒܝܬܐ.
ܘܐܘܟ ܒܝܬܐ ܐܚܪܝܐ ܠܦܘܬ ܒܝܬܐ. ܘܐܠܗ̈ܝܬܐ ܠܟܢ̈ܫܐ ܐܝܟ ܟܢܫܐ. ܘܙܒܢܐ
ܠܢܘܚܐܐܝܟ ܟܢܫܐ. ܘܡܥܙܬܐ ܐܝܟ ܟܢܫܐ. ܘܪܦܙܐ ܠܦܘܬ ܒܝܬܐ ܘܐܠܗܐ ܫܢܝܢ
ܠܦܘܬ ܒܝܬܐ ܘܡܥܙܬܐ ܘܡܘܬܐ ܐܝܟ ܟܢܫܐ܀
ܟܘ ܒܙܡܢܐ ܘܒܙܘܟܠܐ ܚܝܐ ܘܗܕܪܐ ܘܗܠܐ ܠܢܘܚܠܗ* ܘܡܡܠܟܘܗܝ ܘܗܕܪܐ
ܘܗܠܐ ܠܫܘ̈ܩܐ ܘܡܘܬܐ ܠܢܘܚܠܐ. ܘܗܘܠܐܐ ܐܝܟ ܟܢܫܐ. ܘܟܠܗܝܢ ܒܝܬܐ ܩܕܡܝܐ
ܠܡܠܟܐ ܠܐܠܗܐ. ܘܐܘܪܚܐ ܠܫܘ̈ܩܐ ܘܐܠܗ̈ܝܬܐ ܠܟܢ̈ܫܐ. ܙܒܢܐ ܠܢܘܚܐ ܘܐܘܟ
ܠܡܕ̈ܝܢܬܐ ܘܒܝܬܐ.

In *Sapro*: *'enyono* and *sedro* are common; *qolo* and *quqliun* for the martyrs, and *qolo* and *bo'utho* common. Third hour for the martyrs; sixth hour for the Eucharist (*qudoshe*);[10] and the ninth hour for the departed.

Saturday *Ramsho*: *'enyono* and *sedro* are common; *qolo* and *quqliun* for the departed, (also) *qolo* and *bo'utho* for the departed. In *Lilyo*, first nocturne for Theotokos; second for the martyrs; third for the departed and the fourth common, and also of the saint of the (local) church.

And in *Sapro*: *'enyono* and *sedro* common; *qolo* and *quqliun* of the priests, and *sedro* (also) for priests; *qolo* and *bo'utho* (also) for the priests, for on Saturday *Sapro* the priest should be commemorated; the *bo'utho* which is of the priest also indicates this: "O Christ the Bridegroom, call your ministers out of perdition". Again at the third hour the *sedro* is for the priests, (as well as) *qolo*, and *bo'utho*. Sixth hour and ninth hour as usual.

Sunday dawn is a dominical feast, that is Sunday, **[14]** a great day, the beginning of all feasts, and the day of salvation, and of joy and exaltation, because the children of the Church have been held worthy to rejoice and to exult with Christ, their Lord: with him they are not in need of interceders or advocates, but they converse face to face with God, and they honor, magnify and praise Him like the angels who stand near to Him.

---

10 Lit. 'Holy Things; consecrations'.

ܘܒܨܦܪܐ ܚܙܝܬ ܘܫܒܪܐ ܓܘܢܐ ܘܩܠܐ ܘܣܘܣܡܟܠܗܘܢ ܕܫܘܪܐ ܘܗܠܐ ܬܘܒ ܘܟܒܘܬܐ
ܓܘܢܐ. ܘܐܬܟܠܟܠܝܢ ܟܗܘܪܐ. ܘܟܡܐ ܗܟܝܢ ܟܗܘܪܬܐ. ܘܐܬܦܢ ܗܟܝܢ
ܟܟܢܝܫܐ܀
ܘܨܡܐ ܕܟܟܠܐ: ܚܙܝܬ ܘܫܒܪܐ ܓܘܢܐ ܘܩܠܐ ܘܣܘܣܡܟܠܗܘܢ ܕܟܢܝܫܐ. ܗܠܐ ܘܟܒܘܬܐ
ܟܢܝܫܐ. ܘܟܠܠܐ ܟܕܝܐ ܡܕܡܐ ܟܢܟܕܐ ܠܠܗܐ. ܘܐܪܘܝܐ ܟܗܘܪܐ. ܘܐܬܟܠܬܐ
ܟܢܝܫܐ. ܘܪܟܝܟܐ ܓܘܢܗ. ܘܐܘܒ ܟܡܕܝܢܬܐ ܕܐܝܟ ܟܕܝܐ.
ܘܒܨܦܪܐ ܚܙܝܬ ܘܫܒܪܐ ܓܘܢܗ. ܘܩܠܐ ܘܣܘܣܡܟܠܗܘܢ ܕܟܘܐ. ܘܫܒܪܐ ܟܟܘܐ.
ܘܐܘܒ ܗܠܐ ܘܟܒܘܬܐ ܟܟܘܐ. ܡܟܠܠ ܕܒܨܦܪܐ ܕܟܟܠܐ ܕܠܟܗܘܢ ܟܘܐ ܪܘܚ.
ܘܡܗܘܕܐ ܟܗܘܪܐ ܟܒܘܬܐ ܕܟܘܐ ܕܐܬܠܝܗ. ܝܠܬܐ ܡܢܝܚܐ ܡܢܗ ܟܡܟܩܝܢ ܡܢ
ܐܟܕܐ. ܘܟܠܟܠ ܗܟܝܢ ܬܘܒ ܟܟܘܐ ܫܕܪܐ ܘܗܠܐ ܘܟܒܘܬܐ. ܘܟܡܐ ܗܟܝܢ
ܘܟܠܟܠ ܐܝܟ ܟܢܝܫܐ܀
ܕܢܚܘ ܡܢ ܟܡܟܐ ܕܐܬܝܬܡܟܐ ܡܪܝܐ. ܗܘܐ ܡܘܡܐ* ܕܡܢ ܟܡܟܐ ܡܘܡܐ ܪܟܐ
ܐܬܝܗܘܢ ܪܡܐ ܕܦܠܟܘܬܗܘܢ ܟܠܗܘܢ. ܡܘܡܐ ܕܦܘܪܫܢܐ ܘܕܝܢܘܬܐ ܘܪܘܪܐ ܐܬܬ. ܡܟܠܠ
ܕܐܬܝܗܘܢ ܟܢܝ ܟܕܬܐ ܟܡܢܝܐ ܘܟܡܪܘܪ ܟܡ ܡܪܘܗܝ ܡܡܝܢܐ. ܘܗܠܐ ܫܢܡܩܡ
ܟܗ ܟܠܠ ܡܬܟܩܫܐ ܐܘ ܟܠܠ ܫܝܠܓܬܐ: ܐܠܐ ܐܩܡ ܟܐܩܡ ܟܢܡ ܟܡ ܠܠܗܐ
ܘܡܡܢܝܢ ܘܡܘܪܟܡ ܟܗ ܘܡܡܟܝܢ ܐܝܟ ܡܠܐܩܐ ܡܬܐܩܪܟܐ ܕܡܟܗ.

Since for the past six days the priests, deacons and the children of the Church have supplicated the Theotokos and sought the advocacy of the holy martyrs, by [their] prayers and advocacy they were held worthy of seeing the divine majesty, and to rejoice with it as guests in the feast of the King and to be united with Him in joy and exultation, having gained confidence to speak with Him face to face. Because by the prayer of the Theotokos and the holy martyrs they were purified and became pure, they have been held worthy to speak with the Pure One unceasingly and to magnify and glorify Him as he said: “Pure to the Pure One and the luminous to the Luminous One’.

Again it is said: “Blessed are the pure in heart, for they will see God” (Matt. 5:8). When a person purifies themselves, they will see God and will rejoice with Him; otherwise **[15]** their joy will be turned into lamentation, and it will be said to him why did you enter here not having clothing suitable for the feast? And the king will give orders to bind his hands and legs and send him into the outer darkness, while the guests shall have eternal joy with their Lord forever (cfr. Matt. 22:1–14).

11. *Explanation of the services of Sunday*:

[From] the great dominical [feast] of the salvific Resurrection to the *Qudosh ‘edto*, resurrection is celebrated on this great day. The ordering is as follows: On Sunday *Ramsho* they say the *‘enyone, sedre* and *qole* suitable to the resurrection, and its *hulolo* and *pethgomo*. The Gospel is read followed by *quqliun* of the departed and *sedro, qolo, bo’utho* of the resurrection. And *Sutoro* as usual in the tone of the day.

ܡܛܠ ܕܒܩܘܫܬܐ ܐܡܬܐ ܕܒܒܪܗ ܐܬܡܣܟ ܒܩܘܒܐ ܘܡܡܫܡܫܢܐ ܘܚܝܠܐ ܕܒܝܬܐ
ܠܡܠܟܐ ܐܠܗܐ ܘܐܫܬܠܛܘ ܒܫܘܪܐ ܡܕܝܢܬܐ. ܘܒܬܫܒܘܚܬܐ ܐܘ ܒܫܘܠܛܪܘܬܐ
ܐܬܠܘܢ ܠܫܡܝܐ ܠܪܘܡܐ ܐܠܗܘܬܐ. ܘܠܫܡܝܐ ܒܫܡܗ ܐܝܟ ܗܘܝ ܕܐܬܓܠܝܘ
ܒܫܡܝܘܬܐ ܕܡܠܟܐ ܘܐܬܝܚܕܘ ܒܫܡܗ ܒܚܕܘܬܐ ܘܟܪܘܙܐ ܘܫܡܗ ܦܪܘܫܐ
ܕܡܠܟܘܬܗ ܒܫܡܗ ܐܩܝܡ ܠܐܩܝܡ. ܡܛܠ ܕܒܪܟܬܐ ܕܡܠܟܐ ܐܠܗܐ ܘܦܩܘܕܐ
ܡܕܝܢܬܐ ܐܬܕܟܪܘ ܗܘܘ ܘܩܢܐ ܘܐܬܠܘܢ ܕܒܗ ܕܟܠ ܕܡܠܟܘܬܗ ܘܠܐ ܡ̈ܠܟܐ ܠܗ
ܢܡܪܡܘܢ ܘܢܫܒܚܘܢ ܐܒܘܢ ܕܐܡܪ: ܕܟܠ ܠܒܟܠ ܘܚܝܠ ܠܚܝܠܐ.
ܘܐܘܦ ܐܡܪ: ܠܬܠܡܝܕܘܗܝ ܠܐܡܬܝ ܕܕܝܢ ܠܚܠܘܢ ܕܗܘܝ ܚܢܘܢ ܠܐܠܗܐ. ܐܡܠܟ
ܕܒܢܝܐ ܢܕܟܐ ܢܫܡܘ ܚܕܐ ܠܐܠܗܐ ܘܚܕܐ ܒܫܡܗ. ܐܝܟ ܠܐ ܠܐܠܗܐ* ܠܐܬܘܦܢ
ܚܕܘܬܐ. ܘܠܐܡܪ ܠܗ ܡ̈ܠܟܘܬܐ ܒܟܠ ܠܡܘܬܐ ܒܗ ܠܐ ܐܢܬ ܒܟܠܗ ܠܟܘ̈ܠܗܘܢ
ܕܢܫܝܢ ܠܫܡܝܐ ܘܬܫܡܫܘܢ ܡܠܟܐ ܕܠܐܦܝ̈ܗ ܐܬܕܘܢ ܘܩܘ̈ܪܒܢܐ
ܘܬܫܡܫܘܢ ܠܫܡܝܐ ܟ̈ܢܫܐ. ܗܘܝ ܡܛ̈ܝܒܐ ܚܕܘܬܐ ܠܒܫܡܝܐ ܢܚܝܡ ܒܗܘܢ
ܡܪܘܡܝܢ ܕܠܐ ܫܘܠܡ܀
11. ܢܘܗܪܐ ܡܛܠ ܠܫܡܫܐ ܕܚܒܝܒܐ:
ܡܪܢܐ ܙܟܐ ܕܫܡܫܐ ܦܪܘܫܬܐ ܒܝܬܐ ܠܫܘܒܚ ܒܝܬ ܠܫܡܫܐ
ܡܫܡܫܢܘܬܐ ܫܡܐ ܙܟܐ. ܘܬܫܒܘܚܬܐ ܗܘܝܐ ܐܬܠܘܗܝ. ܒܪܫܡܐ ܕܚܝ ܒܫܡܐ
ܐܦܪܝܡ ܒܢ̈ܝܐ ܘܫܒܩܐ ܘܩܠܐ ܕܢܫܚܝܢ ܠܫܡܫܐ. ܘܗܘܐ ܘܩܠܝܠܬܐ ܕܡܠܟܗ.
ܘܦܪܝܡ ܐܘܪܫܠܡ ܘܒܠܘܬܗ ܫܘܡܠܝܗ ܠܒܢ̈ܝܐ. ܘܫܒܩܐ ܘܩܠܐ ܘܒܠܘܬܐ
ܠܫܡܫܐ. ܘܫܘܬܐܐ ܐܝܟ ܒܢܝܐ ܒܗ ܒܫܡܝܐ ܕܩܘܫܐ.

And in *Lilyo*, first nocturn (*edono*), *m'irono*, *sedro*, *qolo* and *bo'utho* of resurrection; second nocturn for the resurrection; third nocturn for the departed; and the fourth is common as in the case of the rest of the days – so as not to omit the common (prayer) of six hours of Sunday night.[11] After it, *quqliun* of the Theotokos, *sedro*, *qolo* – again so as not to omit commemoration of Holy [Theotokos ?]. **[16]**

On the day and at the end, we say the common *bo'utho* because we say two *bo'wotho* of resurrection in the first and second nocturn. In *Sapro*: *'enyono*, *qonuno*, and *sedro* and *qolo* are common – so that the common *sedro* will not be omitted on any morning. The common (*sedro*) shall be completed and then that of the *Theotokos*, *quqliun*, *sedro*, *qolo* and *bo'utho* of the Resurrection. And after having completed (them), they say *quqliun*, *sedro* and the *qolo* of the departed, for it is right that the departed should be commemorated on Sunday, because Christ the King is preparing (a feast) and they rejoice (in it) as guests. *Bo'wotho* are received because (the departed) have become the reason for our existence (?). It is meet that we should be their commemoration, so that we may find compassion before God.

In the third hour, *sedro*, *qolo* and *bo'utho* are on resurrection. In the sixth hour, *sedro*, *qolo* and *bo'utho* are common. In the ninth hour *sedro*, *qole* and *bo'utho* are for the departed, for on all it is appropriate that the departed be commemorated at the ninth hour, because at that time on the Friday of crucifixion our Lord descended towards the departed and visited them, rescuing them from the authority of Satan and consoling them; and he said 'Whenever you are commemorated by your children in the ninth hour in which I entered into your place, **[17]** I remember you, and I give you rest'. For this reason there should be a commemoration of the departed at the ninth hour all days forever, so that they may have mercy from God in the coming world by their commemoration in the Church.

---

[11] That is *Ramsho*, *Sutoro*, and four nocturns of *Lilyo*.

ܘܒܠܠܝܐ ܥܒܝܕܐ ܩܕܝܫܐ ܡܥܒܕܢܝܬܐ ܘܫܦܝܪܐ ܘܡܠܝܐ ܘܡܥܕܪܢܐ ܠܡܫܡܫܢܘܬܐ. ܘܥܒܝܕܐ ܠܐܘܪܚܐ ܠܡܫܡܫܢܘܬܐ. ܘܥܒܝܕܐ ܠܐܟܣܢܝܐ ܠܟܪܝܗܐ. ܘܪܚܝܡܐ ܠܟܠܢܫ ܐܝܟ ܐܒܐ ܕܡܘܗܒܬܐ ܕܠܐ ܢܚܫܠ ܠܟܠܢܫ ܕܢܥܠ ܥܡܗ ܕܟܠܐ ܕܐܝܬ ܠܟܠ. ܘܟܕ ܗܘܐ ܡܫܡܫܢܘܬܗ ܠܡܕܒܪ ܠܟܠ ܘܫܦܝܪܐ ܘܡܠܝܐ ܕܐܝܟ ܠܐ ܢܚܫܠ ܥܡܘܕܗ ܕܡܫܡܫܬܐ ܥܡܗ*

ܥܡܘܕܐ ܕܡܘܟܟܐ ܐܦܪܝܡ ܥܡܕܐ ܠܟܠܢܫܐ. ܡܛܠ ܕܠܡܫܡܫܢܘܬܐ ܐܬܒܪܝ ܠܐܘܪܚ ܟܘܗܢܐ ܥܒܝܕܐ ܩܕܝܫܐ ܘܠܐܘܪܚܐ. ܘܥܪܦܐ ܥܢܝܐ ܘܡܣܟܢܐ ܘܫܦܝܪܐ ܠܟܠܢܫ ܘܟܠ ܕܠܐ ܢܚܫܠ ܫܦܝܪܐ ܠܟܠܢܫ ܕܪܦܐ ܕܦܠܚܘܗܝ ܪ̈ܦܐ. ܙܒܢ ܕܢܬܟܠܠ ܠܟܠܢܫ ܘܟܠܙܒܢ ܠܢܦܫܐ ܠܐܠܗܐ ܘܡܫܡܫܢܘܬܗ ܘܫܦܝܪܐ ܘܡܠܝܐ ܘܡܥܕܪܢܐ ܠܡܫܡܫܢܘܬܐ. ܘܟܠܙܒܢ ܕܡܫܡܫܢܘܬܗ ܐܦܪܝܡ ܡܫܡܫܢܘܬܗ ܘܫܦܝܪܐ ܘܡܠܝܐ ܠܟܪܝܗܐ ܕܥܡܘܕܐ ܕܥܡ ܥܡܕܐ ܙܒܢ ܕܠܟܠܗܘܢ ܟܪܝܗܐ ܡܛܠ ܕܡܫܡܫܢܘܬܐ ܡܥܒܕܢܝܬܐ ܡܛܠܗ ܘܡܣܟܢܐ ܢܦܫ. ܘܥܘܕܪܢܐ ܡܬܟܢܫ ܡܛܠ ܕܗܘܘ ܥܡܗ ܐܬܟܠܝ. ܙܒܢ ܕܗܘܐ ܥܡܗ ܥܘܕܪܢܗܘܢ ܕܠܡܣܟܢܐ ܡܢܗ ܠܐܠܗܐ.

ܘܟܠܗ ܡܢܗ ܫܦܝܪܐ ܘܡܠܝܐ ܘܡܥܕܪܢܐ ܠܐܘܪܚ ܠܡܫܡܫܢܘܬܐ. ܘܟܡܐ ܡܢܗ ܫܦܝܪܐ ܘܡܠܝܐ ܘܡܥܕܪܢܐ ܠܟܘܠܗ. ܘܟܠܗܘܢ ܡܢܗ ܫܦܝܪܐ ܘܡܠܝܐ ܘܡܥܕܪܢܐ ܠܟܪ̈ܝܗܐ ܕܦܠܚܘܗܝ ܡ̈ܣܟܢܐ ܥܢܝܐ ܠܟܪ̈ܝܗܐ ܠܟܠܗܘܢ ܡܢܗ ܢܐܐ ܥܘܕܪܢܐ. ܡܛܠ ܕܥܡ ܥܡܘܕܐ ܥܡܘܕܐ ܕܥܘܕܪܢܐ ܕܡܫܡܫܢܘܬܐ ܚܝܠ ܡܢܗ ܙܕܝܩܘܗܝ ܕܟܪ̈ܝܗܐ ܘܫܦܝܪ ܐܝܟ ܘܡܥܕܪ ܐܝܟ ܡܢ ܡܘܟܟܗ ܕܫܦܝܪܐ ܘܡܥܕܪ ܐܝܟ ܘܐܡܪ ܦܠܚܐ ܕܡܫܡܫܢܘܬܗ ܡܢ ܟܪ̈ܝܗܐ ܥܡܗܘܢ ܥܡܕܐ ܠܐܘܪܚܐ ܕܥܡ ܟܠܗ ܠܟܘܠܗܘܢ:* ܡܫܡܫ ܐܢܐ ܠܗܘܢ ܘܡܥܕܪ ܐܢܐ ܠܗܘܢ. ܟܠ ܗܢܐ ܗܘܐ ܕܥܒܕ ܠܟܪ̈ܝܗܐ ܥܡܘܕܐ ܠܡܫܡܫܢܘܬܐ ܕܦܠܚܘܗܝ ܡ̈ܣܟܢܐ ܠܟܠܗܘܢ: ܕܠܡܫܡܫܢܘܬܗ ܡܢ ܠܐܠܗܐ ܥܡܘܕܐ ܕܟܠܗ ܥܘܕܪܢܗܘܢ ܕܥܕܬܐ܀

12. [*On Sunday*]: Those who make pretexts and confusion ask why is Sunday the beginning of the days, seeing that it did not come to be the first (day) to be mentioned, but has come last, after the (other) six days? This is erroneous and ignorant. The one who affirms should be attentive.

We say rather: even when someone strives to speak of anything temporal, without having seen or understood it (he cannot do so, whereas this)[12] does not come under the bounds of time, because 'the first day', which you spoke of, is not known (to anyone) apart from God alone, its Creator. Whereas we were not speaking of the day which came into being before we came into being, but about the eighth day after our creation, which we observe and we commemorate at the conclusion of the days of the week, and not concerning the day which was after our creation. And we honour Sundays, not as the first day of the dispensation of our Lord, but because of the honour of the great Sunday of Resurrection that shone out for us at the conclusion of the dispensation, **[18]** and on it we see light after the darkness that was with us; on it we have found joy after our griefs.

Since Sunday is the last day, it is the conclusion of this world and the beginning of the coming world. Therefore we make the memory of Sunday in the conclusion of the (other) days, after the dispensation, because in it the griefs have come to an end and joy has been renewed.

Again it is not right that the king comes from distant places without envoys or messengers; rather, the envoys and the messengers come first, then the forces and the camps, the horses and the chariots, and (finally) the king should come. Therefore we left mention of Sunday (until) after the (other) days, coming last, like the king, for he is the 'king of the days' and all souls yearn to see his beauty and to rejoice in his bridal chamber and take delight in his blessings forever and ever.

---

[12] It would seem that some words have been lost (Brock).

12. ܡܬܬܠܠܢܐ ܘܡܬܦܫܩܢܐ ܐܡܪܝܢ. ܡܛܠ ܗ̇ܢܐ ܐܝܟܢܐ ܕܚܕ ܒܪܢܫܐ ܚܛܝܬܐ ܘܡܘܬܐ ܐܟܘ̄. ܘܠܐ ܐܬܐ ܡܘܬܐ ܠܥܠܡܐ ܐܠܐ ܗܘܐ ܐ̱ܢܫܐ ܒܠܚܘܕ ܥܠܬܐ ܡܘܬܐ. ܗܘܐ ܠܡܘܬܐ ܐܡܝܢܐ ܘܠܐܒܝܕܘܬܐ. ܙܕܩ ܕܢܬܐܡܪ ܐܡܘܪܐ.

ܘܐܡܪܝܢ ܕܐܦ ܟܕ ܒܪܢܫܐ ܡܪܐ ܕܢܬܩܛܠ ܥܠ ܡܕܡ ܙܕܝܩܐ ܘܠܐ ܚܛܝܘܗܝ ܘܠܐ ܐܬܬܟܝܠܘ ܐܦܠܐ ܥܠ ܐܢܫܝܢ ܐܚ̈ܪܢܐ ܕܝܢܐ. ܡܛܠ ܕܡܘܬܐ ܡܕܡܐ ܕܐܡܪܬܘܢ ܡܫܬܠܛܐ ܠܐ ܡܫܬܡܗܐ ܐܠܐ ܠܐܠܗܐ ܒܥܘܕ ܒܪܘܚܗ. ܘܥܠ ܠܐ ܡܫܬܠܛ ܥܠ ܡܘܬܐ ܕܗܘܐ ܡܢ ܡܕܡ ܕܗܘܐ ܐܠܐ ܥܠ ܡܘܬܐ ܠܐܢܫܐ ܕܥܠܡܐ ܒܪܢܫܐ. ܘܥܠܗ ܐܡܝܪܐ ܘܠܗ ܒܗܕܐ: ܒܡܘܬܗ ܡ̈ܘܬܐ ܕܒܐܝܕܐ. ܘܠܗ ܡܛܠ ܡ̈ܘܬܐ ܕܗܘܐ ܥܠܘ ܒܪܢܫܐ. ܘܥܠܝܢ ܒܡ̈ܠܐ ܡܫܬܪܝܢ ܘܠܐ ܡܛܠ ܚܕ ܒܡܘܬܐ ܕܒܝܫ̈ܐ ܡܬܒܪܝܢܘܬܗ ܕܡܪܢ ܐܠܐ ܡܛܠ ܐܡܪܐ ܕܚܕ ܒܡܘܬܐ ܙܕܩܐ ܘܡܫܝܚܘܬܐ ܕܒܡܘܬܗ ܡܬܒܪܝܢܘܬܐ ܕܡܫܝܚ* ܠܢ. ܘܠܗ ܚܕܝܢ ܢܗܘܪܐ ܥܠ ܚܝ̈ܘܬܐ ܕܗܘܐ ܠܢ. ܘܠܗ ܐܡܫܝܚ ܡܬܚܘܬܐ ܥܠ ܒܢ̈ܝܢ.

ܘܡܛܠ ܚܕ ܒܪܢܫܐ ܕܡ̈ܘܬܐ ܐ̱ܢܫܐ ܘܐܠܗܘܬܐ ܒܡܘܬܐ ܕܒܪܢܫܐ ܗܘܐ ܘܡܘܬܐ ܕܒܪܢܫܐ ܕܥܠܡ. ܥܠ ܗܕܐ ܐܠܗܝܢ ܒܡܘܕܝܬܐ ܕܚܕ ܒܪܢܫܐ ܒܡܘܬܐ ܡ̈ܘܬܐ ܥܠ ܡܬܒܪܝܢܘܬܐ ܡܛܠ ܕܐܬܟܢܫܘ ܒܗ ܒܢ̈ܝܐ. ܘܐܬܚܝܒܘ ܒܗ ܒܚܝܘܬܐ.

ܐܘܟ ܠܐ ܙܕܩ ܕܢܬܐ ܡܘܬܐ ܡܢܗܝܢ ܡܢ ܐܬܪܘܬܐ ܕܚܛܝܬܐ ܕܠܐ ܐܝܟ ܡܕܡ ܘܠܐ ܡܫܬܪܝܢ. ܐܠܐ ܡܢܗܝܢ ܕܠܐܗ ܐܝܟ ܡܕܡ ܘܡܫܬܪܝܢ. ܘܐܘܟ ܡܫܬܡܠܝܐ ܘܡܫܬܡܠܝܐ ܘܕܡܐ ܘܡܫܬܒܩܢܘܬܐ. ܥܠܝܢ ܕܐܬܐ ܡܘܬܐ. ܥܠ ܗܕܐ ܥܒܕܝܢ ܒܡܘܕܝܬܐ ܕܚܕ ܒܪܢܫܐ ܥܠ ܡܘ̈ܬܐ: ܐ̱ܢܫܐ ܐܝܟ ܡܘܬܐ: ܡܛܠ ܕܗܘܐ ܐܠܗܘܬܐ ܡܘܬܐ ܘܡܘ̈ܬܐ: ܕܢܫܟܚ ܠܗ ܡܘܬܗ ܢܦ̈ܫܬܐ ܕܚܛܝ ܦܠܛܘܗ ܘܚܛܝܢ ܒܡܘܬܗ ܘܐܬܒܫܠܡ ܡܢ ܠܒ̈ܢܝܐ ܒܡܫܝܚܘܬܗ܀

13. *Regulations for the prayer of an entire day, and the prostrations (segdotho) in them and their quantity*: There are ten orders in the ministry of the Holy Church: five among them are ministers – (i.e.) deacons, sub-deacons, chanters, readers and lay people. And five others are those who offer [the *Qurbono*]: Patriarchs, Maphrians, Metropolitans, bishops and [**19**] presbyters.

These ten (orders) are under law and regulations that each of them should fulfill: the ten prayers with their prostrations and the (sign of the) cross, but each one according to his rank and ability. Because deacons and their associates (that is the minor orders) have (to complete) ten prayers a day, that is, daytime and night. There are 150 inclinations (*segdotho*) (to be made) without omission, and with the sign of the cross upon themselves.

First we shall show the regulations regarding the (sign of the) cross. Each one among the ranks of the Church shall stretch forth the forefinger of the right hand and first touch his head, (i.e.) first his forehead and then upon his breast, then on his left shoulder and then his right shoulder in order to complete (the sign of) the cross. This (fore)finger three times indicates the number of the Holy Trinity, because the number three makes one divinity. It is not right that we make (the sign of) the cross with the whole finger, because the Trinity was not crucified. But (only) the tip of the finger shall (touch) the forehead and the breast and the left and the right shoulders.

Again the right (forefinger), because the tip of the finger has a bigger nail [**20**] not like the two others. It (the nail which) resembles the Son who became incarnate in a human body. On the contrary, the Father is the root (*'eqoro*) and the Son is the fruit and the living Spirit is the life of them both. Thus the tip of the forefinger (symbolizes) the Son, (its) lower part the Father, and the middle part the Holy Spirit, who is uniting both of them. Thus it is meet that we shall make the sign of the cross with the tip of the forefinger, which has a nail on it, indicating that one of the *qnume* (hypostasis) was crucified, who is united with a human body.

13. ܬܫܥܝܬܐ ܕܪ̈ܗܛܐ ܕܗܘܘ ܡܫܡܫܢܝܬܐ ܘܥܢ̈ܝܕܬܐ ܕܒܗܘܢ ܘܫܘܫܠܡܗܘܢ:
ܒܫܢ̈ܝ ܡܘܠܟܐ ܐܝܬܝܗܘܢ ܛܒܥܐ ܕܒܝܬܐ ܩܕܝܫܬܐ. ܫܡܗܐ ܕܝܠܗܘܢ ܡܫܡܫܢܐ
ܘܐܝܬܝܗܘܢ: ܡܫܡܫܢܐ. ܐܦܪܝܩܘܣ. ܦܩܠܛܘ. ܐܢܛܝܩܛܘ. ܩܘܠܡܝܢܐ. ܘܫܡܗܐ
ܐ̱ܚܪ̈ܢܐ ܡܫܡ̈ܫܢܐ ܐܝܬܝܗܘܢ: ܦܛܪ̈ܘܣ. ܡܫܡ̈ܫܢܐ. ܡܛܪܘܦܘܠܝܛܐ.
ܐܦܝܣܩܘܦܐ.* ܡܫܡܫܐ.
ܘܗܠܝܢ ܒܫܢ̈ܝ ܡ̈ܠܟܐ ܐܝܟ ܕܠܗܘܢ ܢܛܘܪܘܢ ܘܬܫܥܝܬܐ ܕܟܠܗܝܢ ܕܝܠܗܘܢ ܒܝܢ
ܡ̈ܘܬܐ ܢܗܘܘܢ ܒܫܢ̈ܝ ܪ̈ܗܛܐ ܒܗܘ ܥܢ̈ܝܕܬܐ ܕܡܢܗܘܢ ܘܪ̈ܗܛܐ ܕܒܗܘܢ. ܐܠܐ ܟܠܗܝܢ
ܐܝܟ ܕܪܫܝܡ ܘܐܝܟ ܡܛܠܡܢܝܬܗ. ܡܛܠ ܕܡܫܡܫܢܐ ܘܡܫܡܫܢܘܗܝ ܐܝܟ
ܒܠܗܘܢ ܒܫܢ̈ܝ ܪ̈ܗܛܐ ܒܡܘܬܐ ܚܕ ܐܘܒܕ ܟܠܢܐ ܘܐܬܡܢܬܐ܀ ܥܢ̈ܝܕܬܐ ܡܛܠ
ܘܡܫܡܫܝܢ ܘܠܐ ܒܥܘܕܐ ܒܗܘܢ ܪ̈ܗܛܐ ܕܢܫܡܫܘܢ ܟܠ ܐܦܝܗܘܢ.
ܦܪܫܬܐ ܡܫܡܫܝܢ ܬܫܥܝܬܐ ܕܪ̈ܗܛܐ: ܕܗܘ ܒܟܠܗܘܢ ܡܘܬܒܐ ܒܬ̈ܝܬܐ ܕܦܠܚܝܢ
ܡܫܡܫ ܢܦܘܩ ܚܕ ܪ̈ܗܛܐ ܕܒܠܕ ܒܢܝܬܐ ܕܐܝܬܐ ܕܡܫܡܫܐ ܘܢܦܩܝܢ ܕܡܢܗ ܦܪܫܬܐ
ܒܟܠ ܫܥܬܐ ܘܡܠܬܪܝܢ ܟܠ ܚܝܠܗ ܘܩܡ ܟܠ ܡܠܟܘ ܕܗܫܐ ܘܐܬܐ ܟܠ
ܡܠܟܘ ܕܡܫܡܫܐ ܕܢܬܡܫܠ ܪ̈ܗܛܐ. ܘܗܘܐ ܪܗܛܐ ܕܐܬܡܢ ܬܚܝܬ ܡܫܩܠܬܐ
ܠܡܫܡܫܢܘܬܐ ܦܪܫܬܐ ܪܒܐ. ܡܛܠ ܕܬܚܝܬ ܡܫܩܠܬܐ ܒܫܩܠ ܚܕ ܠܟܠܗܘܢ. ܘܠܐ
ܙܘܥ ܕܒܦܠܚܘ ܪ̈ܗܛܐ ܢܦܩܝܢ ܪ̈ܗܛܐ: ܕܟܠ ܬܚܝܬܘܬܐ ܐܪ̈ܗܛܐ. ܐܠܐ ܙܘܥܐ
ܕܪ̈ܗܛܐ ܢܦܩܝܢ ܒܟܠ ܒܫܥܬܐ ܘܟܠ ܚܝܠܗ ܡܠܟܘ ܕܗܫܐ.
ܬܘܒ ܕܡܫܡܫܢܐ ܡܛܠ ܕܙܘܥܐ ܕܪ̈ܗܛܐ ܐܝܟ ܒܗ ܠܦܘܪܐ ܡܠܟܐ.* ܘܠܐ ܙܡܢܐ ܠܡܠܟܘܬ
ܐ̱ܚܪܢܐ. ܕܕܘܡܝܐ ܕܒܪܐ ܐܝܠܝܢ ܘܐܝܟ ܒܗ ܡܫܬܡܫܢܘܬܐ ܕܦܓܪܐ ܐ̱ܢܫܐ.
ܒܩܘ̈ܦܐ ܕܐܬܐ ܒܫܪܐ ܐܝܠܝܢ ܘܒܪܐ ܦܠܓܐ ܘܙܘܥܐ ܡܛܠ ܕܐܬܘܗܘܢ. ܗܘܝܐ ܪܗܛܐ.
ܙܘܥܐ ܕܡܠܗ ܐܝܟܘ ܒܪܐ ܕܐܬܡܠܐ ܐܬܐ. ܘܡܪܗܛܐ ܙܘܥܐ: ܕܐܝܠܝܢ ܡܬܕܒܪܐ
ܕܐܬܘܗܘܢ. ܒܟܠ ܗܘܝܐ ܙܘܥ ܕܒܙܘܥܐ ܕܪ̈ܗܛܐ ܢܦܩܝܢ ܪ̈ܗܛܐ ܕܐܝܟ ܒܗ ܠܦܘܪܐ.
ܘܡܘܕܥܐ ܕܚܕ ܡܢ ܡܫܩܠܐ ܐܪ̈ܗܛܐ ܕܐܝܟ ܒܗ ܡܬܕܒܪܐ ܒܗ ܦܓܪܐ ܐ̱ܢܫܐ.

Those who make the sign of the cross with two fingers cause suffering to the two *qnume* (hypostases). And if those who make the sign of the cross with two fingers say that is because Christ has two *qnume*, we say: Then you are crucifying two *qnume*, God and humanity. This is an error. And those who make the sign of the cross with three fingers bring the Trinity to passion. They are not right. And if they say, it is because we are sanctifying the Trinity with threefold sanctifications, that we make the (sign of) the cross with three fingers, we say to them: this is worse than the first error. You are making God [**21**] three distinct and separate entities (*dilyotho*). Besides, you are (confessing) three self-existing and distinct entities, by saying: "Holy God the Father, Holy Almighty Son and Holy Immortal Spirit". You are making the Father God, and the Son Almighty and the Spirit Immortal. Each of them has (its own) property apart from the other. It is confirmed by you (when you say) that Father is God, and the Son and Spirit are not Gods; and Son is Almighty and Father and the Sprit are not. The Spirit is immortal, while the Father and the Son are not immortal. This error is worse than the other, (i.e.) the first one.

We say: "Holy art Thou O God", the Son; "Holy art Thou O Almighty", again the Son; "Holy art Thou O Immortal", again the Son. And we make the sign of the cross with the tip of the forefinger and we say, "who was crucified for us have mercy upon us".[13]

---

[13] In the Syrian Orthodox tradition, Trisagion is always understood as addressed to Christ. See S. Brock, "The Thrice-holy hymn in the Liturgy", *SOBORNOST/Eastern Churches Quarterly* (1986), 24–34; Baby Varghese (tr), *The Commentary of Dionysius Bar Salibi on the Eucharist*, (SEERI/Gorgias Press, 2011), ch. 4:5–11.

ܘܗܘ ܕܬܡܫܡܫ ܙܒܢܐ ܒܬܪ̈ܬܝܢ ܙܒ̈ܢܬܐ ܒܬܪ̈ܝܢ ܦܢ̈ܝܬܐ ܡܫܡܫ. ܘܐܦ ܐܡܪܝܢ ܗܘ ܕܒܬܪ̈ܬܝܢ ܙܒ̈ܢܬܐ ܡܙܕܒܢ ܟܠ ܕܐܝܬܘܗܝ ܡܫܝܚܐ ܬܪ̈ܝܢ ܦܢ̈ܝܬܐ ܡܙܕܒܢ ܒܬܪ̈ܬܝܢ. ܘܐܡܪܝܢ ܡܛܠ ܒܬܪ̈ܝܢ. ܦܢ̈ܝܬܐ ܙܒܢܝܢ ܐܝܬܘܗܝ ܠܐܠܗܐ ܘܠܐܢܫܘܬܐ. ܗܘܐ ܠܡܫܘܚܬܐ ܐܝܬܝܗ: ܘܗܘܝ ܕܒܬܠܬܐ ܙ̈ܒܢܬܐ ܢܡܫܚ ܒܬܠܡܝܕܘܬܐ ܠܐܢ̈ܫܝܢ ܚܕ̈ܐ ܡ̈ܢܝܢ ܘܒܟܠ ܐܝܟ ܕܡܢܬܐ. ܘܐܦ ܐܡܪܝܢ ܟܠ ܕܡܬܡܢܝܢ ܒܬܠܡܝܕܘܬܐ ܒܟܠܗ ܦܘܩܕܢܐ ܕܡܫܝܚ ܙܒܢܐ ܒܟܠܗ ܙ̈ܒܢܬܐ. ܘܐܡܪܝܢ ܕܗܘܝ ܗܘܐ ܒܫܡܐ ܡܢ ܡܫܘܚܬܐ ܡܫܡܫܢܘܬܐ ܘܢܚܡܝܘܗܝ ܠܐܠܗܐ* ܬܟܠ ܘܫܒܝܠܐ ܐ̱ܢܫܝܢܝܬܐ ܢܘܡ̈ܘܣܝܬܐ ܡܛܠ ܡܢ ܬܟܠ ܘܫܒܝܬܐ ܐܬܝܢ̈ܝܬܐ ܘܡܫܡܫܢ̈ܝܬܐ ܘܐܡܪܝܢ ܡܢܐ ܠܐܠܗܐ ܐܒܐ. ܡܢܐ ܚܝܠܬܢܐ ܒܪܐ. ܡܢܐ ܠܐ ܡܫܘܚܬܐ ܪܘܚܐ. ܢܗܝܪܘܬܐ ܠܐܒܐ ܠܐܠܗܐ ܘܠܒܪܐ ܚܝܠܬܢܐ ܘܠܪܘܚܐ ܠܐ ܡܫܘܚܬܐ. ܦܠܚܝܢ ܐܢܬ ܠܗ ܘܡܫܡܫܬܐ ܡܛܠ ܡܢ ܐܢܫܐ. ܘܐܬܡܠܟܘܬܐ ܒܥܠܡܐ ܕܐܒܐ ܐܝܬܘ̄ ܐܠܗܐ ܘܒܪܐ ܘܪܘܚܐ ܒܠܚܘܕ ܐܝܟ ܐܠܗ̈ܐ ܘܒܪܐ ܐܝܬܘ̄ ܚܝܠܬܢܐ ܘܐܒܐ ܘܪܘܚܐ ܒܠܚܘܕ ܐܝܟ ܚܝܠܬܢ̈ܝܬܐ. ܘܪܘܚܐ ܐܝܬܘ̄ ܠܐ ܡܫܘܚܬܐ. ܘܐܒܐ ܘܒܪܐ ܒܠܚܘܕ ܐܝܟ ܠܐ ܡܫܘܚܬܐ. ܗܘܐ ܠܡܫܘܚܬܐ ܐ̱ܢܫܝܬܐ ܒܫܡܬܐ ܗܘ ܡܢ ܡܫܡܫܬܐ.

ܘܚܕ ܐܡܪܝܢ ܡܫܡܫ ܠܐܠܗܐ ܒܪܐ. ܡܫܡܫ ܚܝܠܬܢܐ ܬܘܒ ܒܪܐ. ܡܫܡܫ ܠܐ ܡܫܘܚܬܐ ܬܘܒ ܒܪܐ. ܘܡܙܕܒܢ ܒܫܡܐ ܕܒܪܐ ܘܐܡܪܝܢ ܕܐܬܬܒܪܢ ܚܠܦܝܢ ܐܬܪ̈ܚܡܬܢ܀

Thus we speak of the Father who is God and Almighty and Immortal and also of the Spirit we say God, Almighty and Immortal. Everything that the Father has, the Son and the Spirit also have. And everything that the Son has, the Father and the Spirit also have, except generation. And everything the Spirit has, the Father and the Son also have, except procession. These are three distinct properties, apart from them, they have no true ones, only supplementary and foreign.

14. *Again we present the regulations on prostrations* (*segdotho*): Three types of prostrations (*segdotho*) are known: **[22]** the inclination (*rkinutho*) of the neck and the bending (*ghono*) of the back (*ḥaṣo*) and falling down (*gurgoyo*) on the ground. During the *Qurbana*, when the deacon cries out, "Let us bow down our heads [before] the Lord" all the children of the Church should incline (*narken*) their heads. From the salvific feast of Resurrection to Pentecost, as well as in every week of the whole year, they offer the bending of the back (*ghono d-ḥaṣe*). And for the rest of the year, they make the falling down (*gurgoyo*) on the ground, that is prostrating (*sogdin*) on the ground till their [fore]head kiss[14] the ground. Not merely do their hands reach out, but their head touches the earth, and the palms of their hands are folded to worship (*sogdin*), because the hands take the Body and Blood of Christ and the mouths that consume them should not touch the earth, because all human beings and animals tread upon it, (both) pure and impure with their feet.

It is not right for someone to let his body worship and his spirit wander about the created things; rather, both body and spirit should worship together in prayer, so that both shall be received, as it is said in the venerable and holy Gospel, "God is Spirit, and those who worship Him should worship in Spirit and Truth" (John 4:24).

---

[14] *mnšqyn*; but perhaps this is an error for *mnqšyn*, "knock". I am grateful to S. Brock for this comment.

ܗܟܢܐ ܐܡܪܝܢ ܠܐܒܐ ܕܐܝܬܘܗܝ ܐܠܗܐ ܘܡܫܬܟܚܢܐ ܘܠܐ ܡܫܬܢܐ. ܘܐܦ ܒܪܢܫܐ ܐܡܪܝܢ ܐܠܗܐ ܘܡܫܬܟܚܢܐ ܘܠܐ ܡܫܬܢܐ. ܘܦܠܓܝܢ ܕܐܝܬ ܠܐܒܐ ܐܝܬܘ̄ ܒܒܪܐ ܘܒܪܢܫܐ. ܘܦܠܓܝܢ ܕܐܝܬ ܒܒܪܐ ܐܝܬܘ̄ ܠܐܒܐ ܘܒܪܢܫܐ ܗܠܝܢ ܡܢ ܡܚܒܘܬܐ. ܘܦܠܓܝܢ ܕܐܝܬ ܒܪܢܫܐ ܐܝܬܘ̄ ܠܐܒܐ ܘܒܒܪܐ ܗܠܝܢ ܡܢ ܢܩܝܦܘܬܐ. ܗܟܢ ܐܢܫ ܠܒܪ ܕܟܝܢܬܐ ܡܫܡܫܢܝܬܐ. ܘܗܠܝܢ ܡܢܗܘܢ ܠܐ ܐܝܬܝܗܘܢ ܚܕ̈ܝܬܐ ܐܠܐ ܐܘܣܦ̈ܬܐ ܘܢܘܟܪ̈ܝܬܐ܀

14. ܘܐܘܦ ܡܫܡܫܝܢ ܠܐܣܟܡܐ ܕܫܝܢܝܬܐ܆ ܫܝܢܝܬܐ ܒܟܠܟܠܬܐ ܕܬܪܬܐ *ܡܬܝܕܥܝܢ. ܙܟܘܬܐ ܪܒܬܐ ܕܓܘܫܡܐ ܕܚܕܐ ܕܓܘܪܓܡܐ ܕܟܠ ܐܘܪܚܐ. ܐܡܬܝ ܕܡܕܡ ܡܫܡܫܢܐ ܟܕܝ ܡܘܕܟܝܐ ܠܡܪܢܐ ܙ̈ܡܝܢ ܢܦܩ ܙܘܥ ܕܦܠܚܘܗܝ ܒܬܪ ܒܝܬܐ ܢܦܫܗ ܙ̈ܡܝܢܗܘܢ. ܘܡܢ ܟܠܘܐ ܕܡܫܡܫܬܐ ܦܪܘܫܬܐ ܒܝܫܐ ܠܡܫܬܘܫܫܢ ܘܡܦܠܚܘܗܝ ܡ̈ܫܠܐ ܕܟܠܗ ܚܝܠܐ ܓܘܢܐ ܕܬܪܐ ܡܫܪܟܢ. ܘܫܪܟܐ ܕܦܠܚܘ ܚܝܠܐ ܓܘܪܓܡܐ ܟܠ ܐܘܪܚܐ ܚܟܝܡ ܐܘܟܠ ܫܓܝܪ ܟܠ ܐܘܪܚܐ ܕܒܫܠܘܡܘܬܗ ܡ̈ܪܡܬܐ ܠܐܘܪܚܐ ܡܢܫܡܢ. ܐܦܠܐ ܐܢܝܫܘܗܝ ܟܠ ܐܘܪܚܐ ܡܫܠܡ. ܐܠܐ ܡ̈ܪܡܬܗܘܢ ܟܠ ܐܘܪܚܐ ܫܡܫܢ ܘܐܝܬܝܗܘܢ ܟܕ ܡ̈ܦܬܚܢ ܫܓܝܪ ܡܫܠܠ ܕܐܢܝܢܐ ܕܫܩܠܗ ܦܓܪܗ ܘܕܡܗ ܕܡܫܝܚܐ. ܘܦܬ̈ܓܡܐ ܕܐܦܠܗ ܐܢܝ ܠܐ ܙܘܥ ܕܠܐܘܪܚܐ ܢܫܠܘܗܝ ܡܫܠܠ ܕܟܠܡܗ ܕܙܡܢ ܟܠܗܘܢ ܟܢܝܫܐ ܘܡܫܩܠܬܐ ܕܩܢܬܐ ܘܫܩܠܬܐ ܒܪ̈ܓܠܗܘܢ.

ܘܠܐ ܙܘܥ ܠܗ ܠܟܪܝܗܐ ܕܢܫܓܘܗܝ ܦܓܪܗ ܘܟܟܪ̈ܝܬܐ ܠܦܘܐ ܙܘܥܗ. ܐܠܐ ܠܐ̈ܘܡܘܗܝ ܡ̇ܘܠܝܠ ܦܓܪܐ ܘܙܘܥܐ ܒܪܟܬܐ ܢܫܓܝܘܗܝ ܐܡܝܐ ܕܠܐܘܡܘܗܝ ܢܡܡܠܠܘܗܝ ܐܡܠܐ ܕܠܐܐܡܪ ܠܐܘܓܠܗܘܢ ܫܓܝܐ ܘܡܝܬܐ. ܙܘܥܐ ܗ̱ܘ ܓܒܪ ܐܠܗܐ. ܐܝܠܝܢ ܕܫܓܝܪܝܢ ܠܗ ܒܪܢܫܐ ܘܡܥܒܕܐ ܘܠܐ ܕܢܫܓܘܗܝ܀

15. *Beginning of the Prayers and the bowing downs (segdotho) in them and their number*:

First (regarding) the deacons and their associates,[15] each one of the [**23**] five ranks: when the time of the prayer approaches, they shall earnestly stand up and leave their home for the church, in the spirit saying the (following) Psalm: "To You O Lord, I have raised my soul. My God, in You I put trust; let me not put to shame; let not my enemies boast over me; nor let anyone who hopes in You not be put to shame. Let the wicked be [put to shame]. Show me Your ways, O Lord, and make me know Your paths; lead me in Your truth and teach me. For You are my God and Saviour. And every day I wait for you. Remember Your mercies, O Lord and Your graces forever. Remember not the transgressions of my childhood. But according to Your abundant mercies, remember me, because of Your grace, O God" (Ps. 25:1–7).

If he completes the whole psalm, it is good; otherwise he should recite the verses until he reaches the church. If he does not know these verses (by heart), he shall repeat, "Show me Your ways, O Lord, and make known to me Your paths". When he reaches the door of the church on entering, he should say, "It is Your house I have entered, O Lord and before Your throne I have worshipped, O heavenly King. Absolve me every sin that I have committed before You". He shall stand before the altar and purify himself from worldly thoughts, saying:

"Holy, holy, holy Lord Almighty, heaven and earth are full of His glories. Hosanna in the highest". And let him begin, [**24**] "Holy art Thou O God, Holy art Thou O Almighty, Holy art Thou O Immortal, who was crucified for us, have mercy upon us".

---

[15] I.e., the minor orders.

15. ܥܘܪܐ ܕܪ̈ܡܬܐ ܘܫܬܐܣܬܐ ܕܒܗܝܢ ܘܥܡܘܪ̈ܝܗܝܢ:
ܡܝܩܪܐ ܕܡܫܡܫܢܐ ܘܬܫܡܫܬܗܘܢ ܦܠܝܓ ܡܢ* ܘܠܝܡ ܣܓܝ̈ܐܐ ܡܘܬܪ̈ܬܐ. ܐܡܠܟ
ܕܗܘܐ ܒܝܬܐ ܕܪ̈ܡܬܐ: ܡܫܬܠܡܢܐ ܢܣܘܡ ܒܬܐ ܡܢ ܒܣܐܐ ܠܒܝܬܐ ܘܐܡܪ ܒܪܘܚܐ
ܡܫܡܗܘܐ ܒܗܐܝ ܡܪܝܐ ܢܫܡܥ ܐܘܪܫܟ. ܐܠܗܐ ܒܝ ܫ̈ܒܪܐ ܠܐ ܐ̂ܒܗܐ ܘܠܐ
ܢܬܒܗܘܢ ܒܟܐ ܒܒܟܝ̈ܬܐ. ܐܦ ܒܠܐ ܕܡܬܩܪܒ ܒܝ ܠܐ ܢܒܗܬ ܟ̈ܠܠܐ
ܒܬܫܒܘܚܬܗܘܢ. ܐܘܪܚܬܟ ܡܪܝܐ ܚ̈ܘܝ. ܘܫܒܝ̈ܠܝܟ ܐܠܦܝܢܝ. ܕ̈ܒܪܝܢܝ
ܒܫܪܪܟ ܘܐܠܦܝܢܝ. ܡܛܠ ܕܐܢܬ ܗ̣ܘ ܐܠܗܝ ܘܦܪܘܩܝ. ܘܠܟ ܫ̈ܒܪܬ
ܒܟܠܝܘܡ. ܐܬܕܟܪ ܡܪܝܐ ܪ̈ܚܡܝܟ ܘܛܝܒܘܬܟ ܕܡܢ ܥܠܡ. ܘܣܟ̈ܠܘܬܐ ܕܛܠܝܘܬܝ
ܠܐ ܬܬܕܟܪ ܠܝ. ܐܠܐ ܐܝܟ ܣܘܓܐܐ ܕܪ̈ܚܡܝܟ ܐܬܕܟܪܝܢܝ ܡܛܠ ܛܝܒܘܬܟ ܐܠܗܐ.
ܐܝܟ ܢܨܒܬܐ ܒܟܘ ܡܫܡܗܘܐ ܠܗ ܗܘܐ. ܘܐܠܐ ܦܠܛܝܬܐ ܘܠܝܡ ܢܠܐ ܐܒܘܝ
ܒܪܬܐ ܕܡܬܬܐ ܠܒܝܬܐ. ܘܐܦ ܠܐ ܢܚܬ ܠܗܘܠܝܢ ܦܠܛܝܬܐ ܘܐܡܪ: ܐܘܪܚܬܟ ܡܪܝܐ
ܚ̈ܘܝ. ܘܫܒܝ̈ܠܝܟ ܐܠܦܝܢܝ. ܪ̈ܓܠܬܐ ܕܥܬܐ ܠܬܘܪܐ ܕܒܝܬܐ ܘܡܢ ܕܥܠܠ
ܘܐܡܪ: ܠܒܝܬܟ ܐܠܗܐ ܐܥܘܠ ܘܐܣܓܘܕ ܒܗܝܟܠܐ ܕܩܘܕܫܟ ܡܠܟܐ ܡܫܝܚܐ
ܡ̈ܪܝܐ ܠܟ ܦܠܐ ܕܬܫܒܘܚܬܐ ܠܟ. ܘܩܘܡ ܩܕܡ ܡܕܒܚܐ ܘܐܡܪ ܫ̈ܡܥܘ ܡܢ
ܣܘܩܦܐ ܐ̈ܘܪܚܬܐ ܘܐܡܪ: ܩܕܝܫ ܩܕܝܫ ܩܕܝܫ ܡܪܝܐ ܚܝܠܬܢܐ ܕܡܠܝܢ ܫܡܝܐ
ܘܐܪܥܐ ܡܢ ܫܘܒܚܗ. ܐܘܫܥܢܐ ܒ̈ܡܪܘܡܐ. ܘܐܡܪܐ* ܩܕܝܫ ܐܠܗܐ ܩܕܝܫ
ܚܝܠܬܢܐ ܩܕܝܫ ܠܐ ܡ̇ܝܘܬܐ ܕܐܨܛܠܒ ܚܠܦܝܢ ܐܬܪܚܡ ܥܠܝܢ.

And he shall make the sign of the cross upon himself and prostrate (*nesgud*).[16] And again, "Holy art Thou O God – for us, have mercy upon us"; and he shall make the sign of the cross and prostrate (*nesgud*); and again, "Holy art Thou O God, etc." and prostrate (*nesgud*).[17] And then, "Our Lord, have mercy upon us; Our Lord, have pity and mercy upon us; Our Lord answer us and have mercy upon us. Glory to You, Our Lord; Glory to You, Our Lord; Glory to You, our hope forever". (Then) he shall stand erect, stretching his hands and raising his eyes above, towards the Father and shall say: "Our Father who art in heaven, etc.".

If he is a deacon, (he shall say) the Psalm, "Have mercy upon me O God, according (to Your) grace" (Ps. 51) and make three prostrations (*segdotho*).[18] But if he is not a deacon and he does not know the Psalm, he shall make three prostrations (*segdotho*) and beseech mercies from God and ask for absolution of debts and forgiveness of sins for himself and for all the faithful, and he shall be blessed by (kissing) the Gospel, or by (kissing) the door of the sanctuary and go and shall stand in his place until the prayer is completed.

Then with the whole congregation, he shall say, "Holy art Thou O God, etc.", and shall make the sign of the cross upon himself and prostrate (*nesgud*). And gain "Holy art Thou O God" and make the sign of the cross, **[25]** and prostrate and again "Holy art Thou O God", make the sign of the cross and prostrate. And again, "Lord, have mercy upon us, etc.". And again he shall say, "Our Father who art in heaven" as in the beginning, and shall complete his prayer with nine prostrations (*segdotho*). Thus five prayers of the daytime are completed: at *Ramsho*, *Sapro*, Third, Sixth hour and Ninth hour: each prayer (with) nine prostrations, making 45 prostrations.

---

[16] Or venerate.

[17] Cfr. Bar Hebraeus, *Book of Guides (Hudaya) or Nomocanon*, V:5 (tr. B. Varghese, MOC Publications, Kottayam, 2014, pp. 84–85).

[18] Prostrations after Ps. 51 have now disappeared.

ܘܪܫܡ ܙܩܝܦܐ ܥܠ ܐܦܘܗܝ ܘܢܫܩܗ. ܘܐܡܪ ܡܫܒܚ ܐܠܗܐ [ܡܪܝܐ]
ܣܠܩܝܢ ܐܬܪܫܡܬܘܢ. ܘܪܫܡ ܙܩܝܦܐ ܘܢܫܩܗ. ܘܐܡܪ ܡܫܒܚ ܐܠܗܐ
ܘܡܪܝܐ. ܘܢܫܩܗ. ܘܐܡܪ ܗܟܢ ܐܬܪܫܡܬܘܢ ܗܟܢ ܚܘܣ ܘܪܫܡܬܘܢ. ܘܗܟܢ
ܚܝܢ ܘܪܫܡܬܘܢ. ܗܘܝܐ ܠܟ. ܗܟܢ ܗܘܝܐ ܠܟ ܗܟܢ. ܗܘܝܐ ܠܟ
ܗܟܢ ܠܥܠܡ. ܘܢܣܡ ܬܘܕܝܬܐ ܒܝ ܦܘܡܗ ܐܢܕܘܗܝ ܘܡܬܬܢܝܚܝܢ ܠܟܠ
ܚܢܘܗܝ ܟܠ ܐܚܐ ܘܐܡܪ ܐܟܡ ܕܥܡܡܐ ܘܡܪܝܐ.
ܘܡܬܪܡܐ ܘܐܦ ܡܫܡܫܢܐ ܐܢܬܘܢ ܡܕܡܘܬܐ ܕܪܫܡܬܘܢ ܐܠܗܐ ܐܝܟ ܠܝܠܘܬܐ.
ܘܠܘܬܗ ܗܘܬܝܐ ܢܫܩܘܢ ܠܗ. ܘܐܦ ܠܐ ܐܝܬ ܡܫܡܫܢܐ ܘܠܐ ܚܕ ܠܡܕܡܘܬܐ
ܐܠܐ ܗܘܬܝܐ ܢܫܩܘܢ. ܘܟܕ ܕܫܐ ܡܢ ܐܠܗܐ ܘܢܛܠ ܚܘܫܒܐ ܕܚܘܕܐ
ܘܡܘܟܟܐ ܕܫܦܝܪܐ ܠܗ ܘܠܦܠܚܘܗܝ ܡܬܢܝܚܐ ܘܡܬܒܢܐ ܡܢ ܐܘܪܚܬܗ ܐܘ
ܡܢ ܬܪܥܐ ܕܗܝܟܠܐ ܘܡܕܒܚܐ ܘܢܛܠ ܢܫܡ ܒܕܘܟܬܗ ܒܕܡܐ ܕܡܫܬܡܫܢܐ
ܙܟܘܬܐ.
ܗܝܕܝܢ ܢܐܡܪ ܒܗܢ ܦܠܚܗ ܒܫܡܐ ܡܫܒܚ ܐܠܗܐ ܡܪܝܐ. ܘܡܒܪܟ ܥܠ ܐܦܘܗܝ
ܘܢܫܩܗ. ܘܐܡܪ ܡܫܒܚ ܐܠܗܐ ܘܡܒܪܟ* ܘܢܫܩܗ. ܘܐܡܪ ܡܫܒܚ ܐܠܗܐ
ܘܡܒܪܟ ܘܢܫܩܗ. ܘܐܡܪ ܗܟܢ ܐܬܪܫܡܬܘܢ ܡܪܝܐ ܘܐܡܪ ܢܐܡܪ ܐܒܘܢ
ܕܒܫܡܝܐ: ܐܝܟ ܡܫܡܫܢܐ ܘܡܫܡܠܝܢܐ ܙܟܘܬܗ ܒܠܒܗ ܗܘܬܝܐ. ܗܘܝ
ܐܬܛܦܝܢ ܙܟܘܬܐ ܫܡܥ ܕܐܡܫܐ: ܕܪܚܡܐ ܘܕܪܫܐ ܘܐܬܠܟܡ ܗܘܝܢ ܘܬܪܝܢ
ܗܘܝܢ ܘܐܬܠܝܢ ܗܘܝܢ. ܦܠܐ ܙܟܘܬܐ ܐܝܬ ܗܘܬܝܐ ܦܢܝܢ ܐܘܟܠܝܢ ܘܡܫܡܫ
ܗܘܬܝܐ.

And in *Sutoro* nine (prostrations) and (in *Lilyo*) twenty one, making altogether 75 prostrations. In *Sutoro,* as in the beginning of all prayers, one shall say, "Holy art Thou O God, etc." and make the sign of the cross and prostrate. Likewise, again, "Holy art Thou O God" and prostrate. And again as before, he should prostrate, and (say), "Lord, have mercy upon us, etc."; "Our Father who art in Heaven, etc.", followed by three prostrations as we have said.

And again they finish and say the Psalms, "He who sits in the shelter of the Most High" and "I will lift up my eyes to the hills" (Ps. 91 and 121),[19] and then "Blessed is the honour of the Lord in his place forever" (E. 3:12), "Holy and Glorious Trinity, have mercy upon us", and prostrate. And again, "Blessed is the honour of the Lord from his place forever; Blessed and Glorious Trinity, have mercy upon us". And again (we say), "Blessed **[26]** is the honour of the Lord from his place forever. Holy and Glorious Trinity, have mercy upon us" and prostrate.

And then, "Lord, have mercy upon us; Lord, have pity and mercy upon us; Lord answer and have mercy. Lord, receive our service and prayers and have mercy upon us. Glory be to You, God; Glory be to You, O Creator; Glory be to You, our hope forever. Our Father, who art in heaven". The prayer is completed with nine prostrations and they say, "We believe in One God"[20] and conclude.

---

[19] Elsewhere the author says that prostrations are made after Ps. 91 and 121. See §18, Ms. p. 39.

[20] Creed. The author does not speak of the three prostrations made during the Creed.

ܘܟܗܢܘܬܐ ܠܥܠ. ܒܟܠܠܐ ܚܕܐ ܘܒܗܢܝܢ ܒܢ̈ܝ ܦܠܚܘܢ ܥܒܕܝܢ ܘܢܣܒܘ ܡܫܝ̈ܚܘܬܐ.
ܕܟܗܢܘܬܐ ܐܝܟ ܡܪܢܐ ܕܦܠܚܘܢ ܙ̈ܟܘܬܐ ܕܐܡܪ ܡܫܝܚܐ ܐܠܗܐ ܘܡܪܢܐ ܘܦܪܘܩܢ
ܘܢܚܝܢ. ܠܘܬܗ ܡܢ ܠܗ ܠܡܫܝܚܐ ܐܠܗܐ ܘܢܚܝܢ. ܘܐܦ ܕܒܢܬܐ ܐ̱ܢܫܐ
ܘܢܚܝܢ. ܘܐܦ ܡܪܝ ܐܬܪܣܡܠܠܝܢ ܘܡܪܢܐ ܘܐܒܘܢ ܕܒܫܡܝܐ ܘܡܪܢܐ ܘܒܠܘܗ
ܡܫܝ̈ܚܘܬܐ ܐܠܗ ܐܒܗܐ ܕܐܡܪܝܢ.
ܘܐܡܠܟ ܕܡܫܡܫܝܢ ܕܐܡܪܝܢ ܡܕܡܘܬܐ: ܢܠܒ ܒܗܠܘܬܐ ܘܒܪܝܫܐ. ܘܐܘܝܢ ܒܢ̈ܝ
ܠܗܘܐ. ܘܒܠܘܢ ܡܒܪܝ ܗ̱ܘ ܐܡܪܗ ܕܡܪܢܐ ܡܢ ܐܠܗܐ ܒܒܠܒ. ܠܒܠܡܘܬܐ
ܡܫܝܚܐ ܘܡܡܒܪܟܐ ܐܬܪܣܡܠܠܝܢ ܘܢܚܝܢ. ܘܐܦ ܡܒܪܝ ܗ̱ܘ ܐܡܪܗ ܕܡܪܢܐ
ܡܢ ܐܠܗܐ ܒܒܠܒ. ܠܒܠܡܘܬܐ ܡܫܝܚܐ ܘܡܡܒܪܟܐ ܐܬܪܣܠܝܢ ܘܢܚܝܢ.
ܘܐܦ ܡܒܪܝ* ܗ̱ܘ ܐܡܪܗ ܕܡܪܢܐ ܡܢ ܐܠܗܐ ܒܒܠܒ. ܠܒܠܡܘܬܐ ܡܫܝܚܐ
ܘܡܡܒܪܟܐ ܐܬܪܣܡܠܠܝܢ ܘܢܚܝܢ.
ܘܐܦ ܡܪܝ ܐܬܪܣܡܠܠܝܢ. ܡܪܝ ܚܘܫ ܘܪܣܡܠܠܝܢ. ܡܪܝ ܒܢܝ ܘܪܣܡܠܠܝܢ.
ܡܪܝ ܡܟܠ ܠܫܡܫܐ ܘܙܒܢܐ ܘܐܬܪܣܡܠܠܝܢ. ܫܘܒܚܐ ܠܟ ܐܠܗܐ. ܫܘܒܚܐ
ܠܟ ܒܪܘܟܐ. ܫܘܒܚܐ ܠܟ ܡܪܝ ܒܟܠܢ. ܘܐܒܘܢ ܕܒܫܡܝܐ. ܡܫܠܡܢܐ
ܙܒܘܬܐ ܒܠܚܘܕ ܡܫܝ̈ܚܘܬܐ ܘܐܡܪܝܢ ܡܫܡܫܢܝܢ ܒܢܝ ܐܠܗܐ ܘܡܫܠܡܝܢ.

Again for *Lilyo*, as in the beginning of all prayers: "Holy, holy, holy, Lord Almighty, heaven and earth are full of His glories. Hosanna in the highest" and begin with, "Holy art Thou O God; Holy art Thou, O Almighty; Holy art Thou, O Immortal, who was crucified for us, have mercy upon us" and they should make the sign of the cross upon themselves and kneel down. Again, "Holy art, Thou O God" and kneel down; and again "Holy art Thou O God" and prostrate. "Lord, have mercy upon us (etc.)" and at the completion, stand erect and say, "Our Father who art in Heaven" and after it three prostrations, and (then he) shall stand in his place.

And when the first nocturn (*'edono*) [of *Lilyo*] is completed, he shall say, "Blessed is the honour of the Lord, etc."; make the sign of the cross and prostrate. Again, "Blessed is the honour of the Lord, etc." and prostrate, and "Our Lord, have mercy upon us, etc.", and say, "Our Father who art in heaven" as usual.

[**27**] When the second nocturne is held, one should say, "Blessed is the honour of the Lord, etc.", and prostrate. And again at the time of "(Holy and Blessed) Trinity, etc." one should prostrate and then, "Our Father who art in heaven".

And when the third nocturn (*'edono*) is held, one should say, "Blessed is the honour of the Lord" three times and (make) three prostrations, and "Our Father who art in Heaven". At the end of the fourth nocturn, one should say, "Glory to God"[21] in full, and prostrate three times and after it, "Holy art Thou O God" three times with three prostrations, and "Our Lord, have mercy upon us, etc.", and "Our Father who art in heaven, etc.". All these ten prayers make 21 prostrations. A deacon of the Church ought to make 75 prostrations (in all).

---

[21] *Gloria in Excelsis Deo*, chanted at the conclusion of *Lilyo*. The prostrations after *Gloria* have also disappeared now.

ܠܗܘ ܕܐܠܐ ܐܝܟ ܡܘܬܐ ܕܦܠܓܗܘܢ ܕܟ̈ܘܬܐ ܩܕܝܫ ܩܕܝܫ ܩܕܝܫ ܡܪܝܐ
ܚܝܠܬܢܐ ܕܡܠܝܢ ܫܡܝܐ ܘܐܪܥܐ ܡܢ ܬܫܒܘܚܬܗ ܐܘܫܥܢܐ ܒܡܪ̈ܘܡܐ. ܘܐܡܪ
ܩܕܝܫܬ ܐܠܗܐ ܩܕܝܫܬ ܚܝܠܬܢܐ ܩܕܝܫܬ ܠܐ ܡܝܘܬܐ ܕܐܨܛܠܒܬ ܚܠܦܝܢ
ܐܬܪܚܡܥܠܝܢ. ܘܢܪܫܘܡ ܙܩܝܦܐ ܥܠ ܐܦ̈ܘܗܝ ܘܢܣܓܘܕ. ܘܬܘܒ ܩܕܝܫܬ
ܐܠܗܐ. ܘܢܣܓܘܕ. ܘܬܘܒ ܩܕܝܫܬ ܐܠܗܐ ܘܢܣܓܘܕ. ܘܡܪܢ ܐܬܪܚܡܥܠܝܢ
ܡܫܡܫܢܘܬܗ ܘܢܩܘܡ ܠܘܩܒܠ ܘܢܐܡܪ: ܐܒܘܢ ܕܒܫܡܝܐ ܘܒܬܪܗ ܠܟܠܗ ܡܫܒ̈ܚܬܐ
ܘܢܚܬܘܡ ܒܫܘܒܚܐ ܕܝܠܗ.
ܘܟܕ ܡܫܠܡܠܗ ܚܒܝܐ ܩܕܡܝܐ ܢܐܡܪ ܡܙܡܘܪ ܐܡܪܘ ܕܡܪܝܐ ܘܡܪܝܐ ܘܐܪܟܒ
ܘܢܣܓܘܕ. ܘܬܘܒ ܡܙܡܘܪ ܗ̄ܘ ܐܡܪܘ ܕܡܪܝܐ ܘܡܪܝܐ ܘܢܣܓܘܕ ܘܡܪܢ
ܐܬܪܚܡܥܠܝܢ ܘܡܪܝܐ ܘܢܐܡܪ: ܐܒܘܢ ܕܒܫܡܝܐ ܐܝܟ ܚܒܪܐ.*
ܘܟܕ ܢܫܠܡܠܗ ܚܒܝܐ ܬܪܝܢܐ ܢܐܡܪ ܡܙܡܘܪ ܗ̄ܘ ܐܡܪܘ ܕܡܪܝܐ ܘܡܪܝܐ ܘܢܣܓܘܕ.
ܘܬܘܒ ܕܙܒܢܬܐ ܬܠܝܬܝܬܐ ܘܡܪܝܐ ܘܢܣܓܘܕ ܘܐܒܘܢ ܕܒܫܡܝܐ.
ܘܟܕ ܢܫܠܡܠܗ ܚܒܝܐ ܬܠܝܬܝܐ ܢܐܡܪ ܡܙܡܘܪ ܗ̄ܘ ܐܡܪܘ ܕܡܪܝܐ ܠܬܠܬܐ ܙܒ̈ܢܝܢ
ܥܠ ܚܕܐ ܣܓܕ̈ܬܐ ܘܐܒܘܢ ܕܒܫܡܝܐ. ܘܡܫܠܡ ܚܒܝܐ ܙܒܢܝܐ ܢܐܡܪ: ܠܬܫܒܘܚܬܐ
ܠܐܠܗܐ ܡܫܡܫܢܘܬܗ. ܘܢܣܓܘܕ ܒܗ ܥܠ ܚܕܐ ܣܓܕ̈ܬܐ ܘܒܬܪܗ ܩܕܝܫܬ ܐܠܗܐ
ܥܠ ܚܕܐ ܣܓܕ̈ܬܐ ܘܡܪܢ ܐܬܪܚܡܥܠܝܢ ܘܡܪܝܐ ܘܐܒܘܢ ܕܒܫܡܝܐ
ܘܡܪܝܐ.ܗܘ̈ܢ ܦܠܓܗܘܢ ܥܠ ܣܓܕ̈ܬܐ ܗܠܝܢ ܒܗܢܐ ܙܒܢܐ ܡܢܗ ܣܓܕ̈ܬܐ ܐܘܣ
ܠܡܫܡܫܢܐ ܕܣܓܕܬܐ ܢܫܠܡ ܐܢܬ.

But if, as a result of some necessity of this world he should happen to be prevented from coming to the church, he should pray where he is – at home, in the vineyard, or on a journey. Four prayers shall be completed in the church: *Ramsho, Lilyo, Sapro* and *Qurbono* and the rest wherever he is found. If there is no place to prostrate (*nesged*), to prevent himself from become proud, he should pray and prostrate in his soul, that is in his heart, and God will receive his prayer. If there is opportunity for prayer, let him leave (it) for another time and let him pray that prayer does not cease altogether, lest it be demanded of him at the hour <of judgement> [**28**] when he has nothing with which to make prostration. And (his) companions have the obligation to pray four times in the church: *Ramsho*, <*Lilyo*>, *Sapro* and *Qurobo*. In case they do not come (or) are unable to come, let them pray the rest of the prayers wherever they are. If they do not know the prayers, without delay they should learn this short prayer and say it at the time of prayer.

It is (as follows): "Have mercy upon us God the Father, Almighty. We praise You; we bless You; we worship You and we beseech You, Lord God, have pity and have mercy upon us". If they do not complete these which we have mentioned, let the nine prostrations that they make at the time of the *Qurobo* rebuke them and teach them that with every prayer there should be nine prostrations.

16. *Explanation of the prostrations (segdotho) during [the celebration of] the Holy Mysteries*:

When the deacon says to the people, "After the peace which has been given, let us bow down (*narken*) our heads before the Merciful Lord", they venerate (*sogdin*) a first time. When the priest says, "Love of God the Father, etc.", they venerate (*sogdin*) a second time. And when the deacons say, "Have mercy upon us God the Father Almighty, we glorify You, etc.", they venerate (*sogdin*) a third time. And when the priest says, "May the Mercies of the Great God, etc.", they venerate (*sogdin*) a fourth time.

ܐܝܟ ܡܠܬܗ ܐܫܠܡܘܬܗ ܕܥܠܡܐ ܗܘܬ. ܡܫܘܚܬܐ ܥܒܕ ܘܠܐ ܢܬܬ ܠܟܝܢܐ ܕܠܐ
ܐܡܬܐ ܕܗܘܐ ܒܟܝܢܬܐ ܒܒܪܝܬܐ ܠܬܘܪܨܐ. ܘܐܪܥܝ ܨܒܝܢܬܐ ܒܟܝܢܐ ܢܬܩܢܘܢ ܘܪܫܡܐ
ܘܟܠܗ ܘܪܩܝܥܐ ܘܡܘܙܠܐ ܘܣܗܪܐ ܐܡܬܐ ܕܡܬܬܠܝܕ. ܘܐܦ ܟܠܗ ܐܬܪܐ ܠܡܬܚܫܒ ܕܠܐ
ܢܬܟܦܪ ܕܠܐ ܘܢܫܟܚܘܢ ܒܫܡܐ ܐܘܟܝܬ ܟܠܟܠ. ܘܐܟܘܬ ܡܫܡܠܝ ܨܒܝܢܗ. ܘܐܦ
ܟܠܗ ܐܬܪܐ ܠܨܒܝܢܬܐ ܢܫܡܥ ܠܟܝܢܐ ܐ̱ܚܪܢܐ ܘܕܠܐ ܕܠܐ ܐ̄ܬܠܒܟ ܨܒܝܢܬܐ ܗ̄ܘ ܕܠܐ
ܢܬܟܢ ܒܡ̈ܬܠܬܐ* ܕܠܐ ܐܝܟ ܒܗ ܡܕܡ ܠܡܫܪܝܘ ܘܢܩܦܐ ܐܬܪܥܝ ܨܒܝܢ̈ܬܐ
ܣܓܝܐܝܢ ܕܨܒܝܢܝ ܒܟܝܢܐ ܙܡܢܐ ܘܪܩܝܥܐ ܘܡܘܙܠܐ ܐܢ ܥܒܕ ܘܠܐ ܢܬܬܘܢ: ܨܒܝܢܝ
ܐܡܬܐ ܕܐܬܚܫܒܘܢ ܒܗ ܨܒܝܢܬܐ ܕܫܪܒܐ ܐܢ ܝܕ ܠܐ ܐܘܕܝܢ ܨܒܝܢ̈ܬܐ ܕܠܐ ܐܦܫܪܐ ܢܬܟܢܘܢ
ܗܘܐ ܨܒܝܢܬܐ ܒܪܝܬܐ ܘܢܬܒܪܘܟ ܒܟܝܢܐ ܕܨܒܝܢ̈ܬܐ ܒܟܝܢܐ ܕܨܒܝܢ̈ܬܐ.
ܘܐܡܪܘ ܐܬܪܡܪܡܢܢ ܠܐܠܗܐ ܐܒܐ ܐܚܝܕ ܟܠ. ܠܟ ܡܫܒܚܝܢ. ܠܟ
ܡܒܪܟܝܢ. ܠܟ ܣܓܕܝܢ ܘܡܘܕܝܢ ܡܛܠ ܡܪܢܐ ܠܐܠܗܐ ܣܘܥ ܘܐܬܪܡܪܡܢܢ.
ܘܐܦ ܠܐ ܢܫܬܠܛ ܠܟܠܢ ܘܐܡܪܝܢ ܫܒܝܚܬܐ ܐܠܗܐ ܕܫܒܝܚ ܒܟܝܢܐ ܕܡܫܘܚܬܐ
ܡܫܡܠܝ ܠܗܘܢ ܘܡܠܝܢ ܕܒܟܠ ܚܕܐ ܨܒܝܢܬܐ ܐܠܗܐ ܫܒܝܚܬܐ ܙܪܥ.
16. ܢܗܘܪܐ ܕܫܒܝܚܬܐ ܒܟܝܢ ܐ̱ܬܪܐ ܡܪܝܡܐ:
ܐܬܟܠܝ ܘܐܡܪ ܡܫܡܫܢܐ ܠܦܠܚܘ ܚܕܐ ܡܢ ܟܠܪ ܗܟܢܐ ܡܪܝܡܐ ܕܐܬܝܗܒ ܡܢܝܢ
ܡܪܝܐ ܡܪܚܡܢܐ ܕܟܝܢ ܢܦܫ ܫܒܝܚ ܚܕܐ. ܘܟܕ ܘܐܡܪ ܒܗܢܐ ܚܘܒܐ ܘܐܟܘܬ ܐܒܐ
ܘܝܡܝܢܐ ܫܒܝܚ ܠܐܘܚܕܢܐ. ܘܟܕ ܐܡܪܝܢ ܡܫܡܫܢܐ ܐܬܪܡܪܡܢܢ ܠܐܠܗܐ ܐܒܐ
ܐܚܝܕ ܟܠ ܠܟ ܡܫܒܚܝܢ ܘܡܪܝܐ ܘܫܒܝܚ ܐܠܗܘܬܐ. ܘܟܕ ܘܐܡܪ ܒܗܢܐ
ܢܗܘܪ ܩܝܡܬܗ ܘܐܟܘܬ ܪܒܐ ܘܡܪܝܐ ܫܒܝܚ ܪܒܘܬܐ.

After the prayer, “Our Father who art in heaven”; and when the deacon says, “Before **[29]** receiving the Holy Mysteries, let us bow down (*narken*) our heads before the Merciful Lord”, they venerate (*sogdin*) a fifth time. When the priest says, “May the grace of the Trinity,” they venerate (*sogdin*) a sixth time and when the priest takes the Holy Mysteries and turns towards the people to give communion, they venerate (*sogdin*) before the mysteries [a seventh time]. And when the deacon says, “After having received the Holy Mysteries, let us bow down (*narken*) our heads before the Merciful Lord, they venerate (*sogdin*) an eighth time. And at the conclusion, when the priest says, “Go in peace, my brethren, etc.”, they venerate (*sogdin*) a ninth time.

These nine venerations (*segdotho*) during the Holy Mysteries are confirmed, for in each (time of) prayer there are nine prostrations (*segdotho*). If these [arguments] are not enough for you, we add (further) testimony from the venerable and Holy Gospel. When our Lord told His disciples: “Amen, I tell you everything that you bind on earth shall be bound in heaven, and everything you loose on earth shall be loosed in heaven” (Matt. 18:18).

Again, “I am telling you if two of you agree on earth about any matter, if you ask, it will be done for you by my Father in heaven, for where two or three are gathered in my name, then am I in the midst of them” (Matt. 18:19–20). Our Lord said **[30]** these words to His disciples by which he ordained them and made them ministers, giving them authority to bind and to loose. He did not give (authority) to bind and to loose as they wish or heedlessly, but when they see some sinner and offender and have rebuked him many times, then if he does not listen, they shall beseech God that he be bound, and they bind him. But if he is obedient and repents about his sins and offences, they shall supplicate God that he may be released, and they release him. Therefore he adds, saying: “If two of you agree on earth about a matter, if they ask, it will be done for them by my Father who is in heaven” (Matt. 18:19).

ܘܒܬܪ ܙܟܘܬܐ ܕܐܒܘܗ̄ܝ ܕܒܫܡܝܐ ܢܐܡܪ: ܡܫܡܫܢܐ ܡܢ ܩܕܡ ܢܫܡܘܬܐ ܕܥܝ̈ܪܐ ܩܕ̈ܝܫܐ ܩܕܡ ܡܪܝܐ ܡܪܚܡܢܐ ܪ̈ܚܡ ܒܢܝ ܫܠܝܡ ܕܗ̄. ܘܒܗ ܕܐܡܪ ܒܘܝܐ ܠܗܘܐ ܠܚܙܘܬܐ ܕܐܠܗܘܬܐ ܫܠܝܡ ܕܗ̄ ܘܟܕ ܫܡܠ ܟܪ̈ܝܐ ܩܕ̈ܝܫܐ* ܘܡܘ̈ܣܦ ܐܦ̈ܝܗܘܢ ܒܗܘ ܒܝܬܐ ܕܢܫܬܘܬܦܘܢ ܫܠܝܡ ܩܕܡ ܥ̈ܝܪܐ. ܘܐܡܠܟ ܕܐܡܪ ܡܫܡܫܢܐ ܡܢ ܒܬܪ ܢܫܡܘܬܐ ܕܥܝ̈ܪܐ ܩܕ̈ܝܫܐ ܩܕܡ ܡܪܝܐ ܡܪܚܡܢܐ ܪ̈ܚܡ ܒܢܝ ܫܠܝܡ ܕܗ̄ ܘܒܬܘܟܠܢܐ ܐܡܠܟ ܕܐܡܪ ܒܗܘܢ ܐܒܘܗ̄ܝ ܒܡܠܟܘܬܐ ܐܚ̈ܝ ܘܡܪܝܐ ܫܠܝܡ ܕܠ̄ܐ. ܗܟܝܠ ܠܗܘܢ ܫܠܝܛܘܬܐ ܕܒܪܝܬܐ ܕܥ̈ܝܪܐ ܩܕ̈ܝܫܐ ܡܫܡ̈ܫܢܐ ܕܐܝܬ ܒܟܠ ܚܕܐ ܙܟܘܬܐ ܠܗܘܢ ܫܠܝܛܘܬܐ ܘܐܢ ܗܟܝܠ ܠܐ ܦܫܩܝܢ ܠܟ ܫܘܒܚܐ ܡ̈ܫܒܚܝܢ ܠܟ ܡܢ ܐܘܪ̈ܚܬܗܘܢ ܫܦܝܪܐ ܘܡܢܝܚܐ ܟܕ ܐܡܪ ܡܪܢ ܠܬܠܡ̈ܝܕܘܗܝ: ܐܡܝܢ ܐܡܪ ܐ̱ܢܐ ܠܟܘܢ ܕܟܠ ܐܝܠܝܢ ܕܐܫܬܘܝܘ ܥܠ ܐܘܪܚܐ ܢܩܘܡ ܐܚ̈ܝ ܒܫܡܝܐ. ܘܟܠ ܐܝܠܝܢ ܕܐܫܬܘܝܘ ܥܠ ܐܘܪܚܐ ܢܩܘܡ ܚܬܝܡ ܟ̈ܡܝܢܐ.

ܠܘܬ ܕܝܢ ܐܡܪ ܐ̱ܢܐ ܠܟܘܢ ܕܐܢ ܠܐܘܝ ܗܘܝܬܘܢ ܢܠܒܫܘܢ ܥܠ ܐܘܪܚܐ ܡܫܬܐܠ ܥܠ ܫܘܒܪܐ ܗܘ ܕܐܢ ܢܫܬܘܕܥܘܢ ܠܟܘܢ ܡܢ ܐܒܐ ܕܝܠܟ ܗܘ ܕܒܫܡܝܐ. ܐܡܬܐ ܫܦܝܪ ܕܐܬܚܙܝܘܢ ܠܘܬ ܐܘ ܠܐܠܗܐ ܕܚܣܝܢ ܟ̈ܡܝܢܐ ܕܝܠܗ ܠܘܬ ܐܝܠܝܢ ܒܡܠܟܘܬܐ ܕܝܠܗܘܢ. ܗܟܝܠ ܡܠܐ ܕܐܡܪ* ܡܪܢ ܠܬܠܡ̈ܝܕܘܗܝ ܒܗܝ ܐܫܪܝܢ ܐܢܘܢ ܘܟܕ ܐܢܘܢ ܡܫܡ̈ܫܢܐ ܘܗܘܘ ܠܗܘܢ ܚܒܪ̈ܝܐ ܕܐܝܬܝܗܘܢ ܘܒܢܝܗܘܢ. ܘܠܐ ܗܘܘ ܕܐܝܬܝܗܘܢ ܘܒܢܝܗܘܢ ܐܝܟ ܕܪ̈ܚܡܝܢ ܐܘ ܐܡܒܠܐ ܐܠܐ ܐܢܫܐ ܕܢܬܡܠܟ ܒܪܢܫܐ ܚܛܝܐ ܘܡܫܡܫܢܐ. ܘܐܡܫܘܚܘܢ ܕܥܝ̈ܪܐ. ܘܐܢ ܠܐ ܡ̈ܫܒܚ ܢܒܥܘܢ ܡܢ ܐܠܗܐ ܕܠܐܠܗܐ ܘܢܫܬܘܬܦܘܢ. ܐܝܟ ܕܠܐܦܫ ܘܢܠܘܒ ܡܢ ܚܛ̈ܗܐ ܘܡܫܡܫܢܘܬܐ ܕܒܥܘܢ ܡܢ ܐܠܗܐ ܕܢܫܬܘܐ ܘܒܢܝܗܘܢ. ܘܡܫܬܠܘܐ ܐܡܪ ܡܪܢ ܕܐܢ ܠܐܘܝ ܡܫܒܚܘܢ ܢܠܒܫܘܢ ܥܠ ܐܘܪܚܐ ܡܫܬܐܠ ܫܘܒܪܐ. ܗܘ ܕܐܢ ܢܬܠܟܘܢ ܢܗܘܐ ܠܟܘܢ ܡܢ ܐܒܐ ܕܝܠܟ ܕܒܫܡܝܐ.

He (Christ) makes known by this that, together with the request, the demand and the ratification, their words will be received, whether they bind or loose. He did not make them people who give commands, but ones who require and ask questions, for they are mediators between God and men. Moreover, he said, when two or three are assembled in my name, I am there in their midst.

By this he made it known that he spoke these words, not specially for the Apostles alone, for he said, "Where they are" and not "Where you are"; rather (he referred) [**31**] to all the ministers who come after them, who are gathered together in the church in the name of the Lord and ask Him mercy on all the children of the Holy Church, Christ being in their midst. Therefore the ministers ought continually to be gathered together in the church, because God made them mediators between the bishops and the people, and through them the sins and iniquities of the people are forgiven.

Its confirmation: when Peter approached Him and asked: "Lord, how many times shall I forgive my brother if he sins against me? As many as seven times? Jesus said to him, "I do not say seven times, but seventy times seven."[22] By saying seven, Simon magnified and glorified himself, because he himself set a limit to the forgiveness of the offences of his brethren. Therefore our Lord replied that he should forgive seventy times seven. A man does not commit offences against his companion seven times a day. If he commits offence two or three times a day, it is reckoned as one offence. But does the utterance of Simon imply, 'if my brother sins against me seven times in seven [**32**] days?' No!

[22] Matt. 18:21–22 (Harklean).

ܡܛܘܠ ܕܗܘܐ ܕܒܗ ܡܠܟܬܐ ܘܐܠܗ̈ܝܬܐ ܘܫܘܪܪܐ ܡܠ̈ܐ ܕܡܠܟܗܘܢ ܠܡܩܒܠܘ ܐܢ
ܢܐܡܪܘܢ ܐܘ ܢܫܪܘܢ. ܕܠܗ ܦܩܘܕܐ ܕܟܕ ܐܝܟ ܡܪܝ ܐܠܐ ܠܐܒ̈ܗܬܐ ܘܡܠܐܟ̈ܐ
ܡܛܠ ܕܡܫܝܚܐ ܐܝܟ ܕܒܗ ܐܠܗܐ ܠܒܢܝ̈ܢܫܐ. ܘܐܘܣܦ ܘܐܡܪ ܐܡܬܝ ܕܝܢ
ܘܐܬܝܬܘܢ ܠܘܬܝ ܐܘ ܠܐܠܗܐ ܕܚܫܒܝܢ ܒܫܡܝܐ ܘܡܢܐ ܠܐܡ ܐܬܐ ܒܡܪܝܬܐ
ܕܡܠܟܗܘܢ.

ܒܗܘܐ ܕܫܘܐ ܕܠܗ ܕܡܠܟܘܬܗ ܠܡܫܝܚܐ ܒܚܝܠܗ ܐܡܪܢܘ ܗܘܐ ܡܠܟܬܐ ܡܢ ܐܡܪ
ܐܡܬܝ ܕܝܢ ܕܐܬܝܬܘܢ ܘܠܗ ܕܐܬܝܬܘܢ ܐܠܐ* ܠܦܠܚܘܢ ܡܫܡܫܢܐ ܕܐܬܐ
ܟ݁ܬܪܘܗܝ. ܐܝܟ ܕܡܬܚܫܒܝܢ ܒܕܝܢܐ ܒܠܠ ܥܡܗ ܕܡܪܝܐ ܘܡܠܟܝܢ ܡܢܗ ܩ̈ܕܝܫܐ
ܠܦܠܚܘܢ ܒܬܝ ܒܕܝܐ ܡܢܝܬܐ ܗܘܐ ܡܫܡܫܢܘܬܗܘܢ.ܡܛܠܗܘܐ ܙܘܦ
ܠܡܫܡܫܢܐ ܘܐܡܝܢܐܝܬ ܢܬܚܫܒܘܢ ܒܕܝܐ ܒܠܠ ܕܡܫܝܚܐ ܒܒܝ ܐܝܟ ܐܠܗܐ.
ܘܚܝܠ ܩ̈ܕܝܫ ܟ݁ܘ̈ܬܐ ܠܒܢܝܐ ܘܠܐܒ̈ܕܝܗܘܢ ܣܓ̈ܝܐܐ ܘܡܫܟܠܬܐ ܕܒܢܝܐ ܡܫܬܠܡܝܢ.
ܡܛܘܪܪܐ ܗܕܝܢ ܡܢ ܡܪܢ ܠܗܐܘ ܦܛܪܘܣ ܐܡܪ ܡܪܢܐ ܟܡܐ ܙܒ̈ܢܝܢ ܐܢ ܢܣܟܠ ܒܝ
ܐܚܝ ܐܫܒܘܩ ܠܗ. ܒܕܡܐ ܠܫܒܥ ܙܒ̈ܢܝܢ. ܐܡܪ ܠܗ ܝܫܘܥ: ܠܐ ܐܡܪ ܐ̱ܢܐ ܠܟ
ܒܕܡܐ ܠܫܒܥ ܙܒ̈ܢܝܢ ܐܠܐ ܒܕܡܐ ܠܫܒܥܝܢ ܙܒ̈ܢܝܢ ܫܒܥ ܫܒܥ. ܗܟܢ ܐܦܘܪܘܣ
ܘܐܬܠܒܘܫ ܫܒܥܐ ܒܥܠܡ ܫܒܥ ܕܐܡܪ ܒܠܠ ܕܕܡܠܟܘܬܗ ܠܐܝܟ ܒܟܠܗ
ܫܘܒܩܢܐ ܠܚܛ̈ܗܝ ܫܬܟܠܬܐ. ܒܬܗܘܐ ܦܝܫ ܡܪܝ ܠܗ ܕܢܫܒܘܩ ܫܒ̈ܩܝܢ ܙܒ̈ܢܝܢ
ܫܒܥ. ܒܠܠ ܕܙܢܝܐ ܠܐ ܡܫܬܟܚܠ ܒܒܪܢܫܐ ܫܒܥ ܙܒ̈ܢܬܐ ܒܝܘܡ ܚܕܐ. ܐܘ
ܡܫܬܟܚܠ ܕܒܢܬܐ ܘܐܬܪܝܡ ܘܐܬܟܠܗ ܒܝܘܡ ܚܕܐ. ܫܒܩ ܫܒܥܬܐ ܡܬܬܐܡܪܐ ܐܠܐ
ܫܒܠܐ ܕܡܫܝܚܐ ܗܘܐ ܫܘܟܠܗ ܠܐܡܬܐ ܐܢ ܢܣܟܠ ܒܝ ܐܚܝ ܫܒܥ ܙܒ̈ܢܝܢ
ܒܝܘܡܐ* ܢܫܡܬܐ ܠܐ.

Rather, the number seven was lauded among those of old. Therefore Simon put a limit 'seven times' with the number seven. Our Lord Jesus Christ – Praised be His grace[23] – did not hold back Simon by what He said, because He saw that he (Simon) had asked reasonably by limiting forgiveness with the small number seven. Rather, with wisdom and kindness, He replied to Simon, saying, "I do not tell to you seven (times), but seventy times seven".

By this response he informed Simon that there are three (groupings of) of (*shabu'o*): a small number seven, (namely) seven; a middling number seven, (namely) seventy and a large number seven (namely) seven hundred. Its meaning is as follows: O Simon, why do you limit forgiveness to the small number seven, and why did you not remember the middle (one) and the large one? You ought not to put a limit to forgiveness. The fact that you yourself have put a limit to your brother (with regard to) the offence, and to yourself for forgiveness is (matter of) pride. It would have been appropriate for you to say, "How often should my brother forgive me if I sin". But you have attributed an offence to your brother and (attributed) to yourself the forgiveness with this small number seven. I am not forcing on you the large number seven, but when [**33**] your brother commits offence against you each week, you are to forgive him seventy times seven times over: every day seventy times, that is the middling number seventy. Do not think I have placed a limit by this number seventy, because a person does not commit an offence seventy times a day. Rather, I have told you, every time he transgresses against you, forgive him, and every time you do wrong, beseech for forgiveness, for there is never despair of repentance until the last breath.

---

[23] This may be an example of the influence of Arabic language on Syriac.

ܡܛܠ ܚܝܐ ܡܚܝܢܐ ܡܫܠܡܘ ܠܗܝ ܡܕܡܝܐ. ܟܠ ܗܢܐ ܡܥܡܕܝ ܗܘܘ
ܐܢܫܐ ܒܡܥܡܘܕܝܬܐ ܕܝܘܚܢܢ. ܡܢ ܫܡܥܘܢ ܡܥܡܕܢܐ ܡܘܗܒܬܐ ܠܡܥܡܘܕܝܬܗ ܠܐ ܕܟܝܢ
ܠܡܥܡܕܘ ܗܘܐ ܕܐܡܪ ܡܛܠ ܕܚܛܗܘܗܝ ܕܗܘܼܢܵܝܬܗ ܥܠܠ ܕܐܝܟ ܡܘܗܒܬܐ
ܒܡܥܡܘܕܝܬܐ ܕܝܘܚܢܢ. ܐܠܐ ܡܬܚܫܒܬܗ ܘܡܫܘܚܠܦܬܗ ܩܕܝ ܘܐܡܪ ܠܡܥܡܕܘ: ܠܐ ܐܡܪ
ܐܢܐ ܠܟܘܢ ܕܢܗܘܐ ܠܡܥܡܕܘ ܐܠܐ ܕܢܗܘܐ ܠܡܬܝܒܝ ܐܚܪܢܐ ܡܢܗ.
ܗܘܐ ܦܘܠܐ ܐܘܕܥ ܠܡܥܡܕܘ ܡܥܡܘܕܝܬܐ ܐܠܗܝܬܐ ܐܝܟ. ܡܥܡܘܕܝܬܐ ܕܝܘܚܢܢ ܡܥܒܕܐ
ܘܡܥܡܘܕܝܬܐ ܡܕܝܢܐ ܡܥܒܕܝܢ ܘܡܥܡܘܕܝܬܐ ܪܒܐ ܡܥܒܕ ܡܠܐ. ܘܫܘܡܠܝܗ ܗܘܝܐ ܗܘ. ܐܘ
ܡܥܡܕܘ ܒܠܥܕܐ ܐܫܡܥ ܠܡܘܗܒܬܐ ܒܡܥܡܘܕܝܬܐ ܕܝܘܚܢܢ ܘܠܐ ܒܗܘܝܐ ܠܡܕܝܢܐ
ܘܒܪܬܐ. ܐܘܕܥ ܗܘܐ ܠܢ ܕܠܐ ܐܫܡܥ ܐܢܫܐ ܠܡܘܗܒܬܐ. ܘܗܘ ܕܕܡܟܝܬܗ
ܐܫܡܥ ܠܐܚܪܢ ܡܥܡܘܕܝܬܐ ܘܠܢ ܡܘܗܒܬܐ ܡܫܘܕܥܐ ܐܝܟܘܬܗ. ܡܛܠ ܗܘܐ ܠܢ
ܕܐܡܪ ܒܡܠܐ ܕܚܝܐ ܐܝ ܡܢܗܠ ܐܢܐ ܡܠܝܚ ܢܡܥܕ ܠܢ. ܐܠܐ ܫܡܥܬ ܠܐܚܪܢ
ܡܥܡܘܕܝܬܐ ܘܠܢ ܡܘܕܝܐ ܒܡܥܡܘܕܝܬܐ ܕܝܘܚܢܢ. ܠܐ ܟܠܝ ܐܢܐ ܠܢ ܠܡܥܡܕܘ ܪܒܐ. ܐܠܐ
ܐܝܟܘ* ܕܡܫܬܟܚ ܒܢ ܐܚܪܢ. ܡܛܠ ܕܝܠܬܐ ܒܡܥܡܘܕܝܬܐ ܐܝܬ ܡܥܡܕ ܠܗ.
ܡܥܡܕ ܕܝܠܬܐ ܡܥܠ ܗܘܝܢ. ܟܠ ܫܘܡܠܐ ܡܥܡܕ ܕܝܠܬܐ ܗ̄ ܡܥܡܘܕܝܬܐ ܡܕܝܢܐ.
ܘܠܐ ܐܫܡܥ ܕܐܢܫܐ ܫܡܥܬ ܗܘܝܐ ܡܢܝܢܐ. ܡܥܡܕܢܐ. ܟܠ ܕܒܪܢܫܐ ܫܡܥ ܠܐ
ܡܫܬܟܚ ܡܩܕܡ ܕܝܠܬܐ ܚܕܐ ܡܘܗܒܐ. ܐܠܐ ܐܡܪܬ ܠܢ ܦܠܚܬܐ ܘܡܫܬܟܚ ܒܢ
ܡܥܡܕ ܠܗ. ܘܦܠܛ ܡܐ ܕܡܫܬܟܚ ܐܝܬ ܒܗ ܡܘܗܒܬܐ ܕܒܬܪ ܦܫܛ ܫܡܥܐ
ܠܬܡܢܬܐ ܕܢܗܘܐ ܒܡܫܬܟܚܬܐ ܐܚܪܢܝܬܐ.

By this he confirmed concerning Simon that whenever he is in the order of ministers, he has a precept that every day he shall venerate (*nesgud*) seventy times and shall forgive and beseech forgiveness for himself, and for the sheepfold of Christ seventy times.

If someone ask whether our Lord set a limit of 'seventy'? Why did the speaker [=author] add five other (prostrations) a day?[24] We say: If we (just) fulfill what we were instructed, what benefit would we have? Rather, we have added the five talents, (so) there is benefit for us.

Again another confirmation from the Holy Gospel: If you forgive people their sins, your Father in heaven also will forgive you. **[34]** "If you do not forgive people their trespasses, neither will your Father forgive you your trespasses (Matt. 6:15)". He showed by his saying "trespass or no trespass" confirming concerning a person forgiving every day seventy times over, and then he may seek forgiveness seventy times.

You may say, perhaps his prayer will be accepted before God. If he forgives and says, 'Forgive us as we also have forgiven', his utterance will be true before God and He will forgive him all his trespasses. But if he does not forgive and says: 'Forgive us as we also have forgiven', his utterance will be a falsehood before God. Would that it just be that he does not forgive him, and not a double wrath upon him from God as he has lied before God; and his prayer will become a sin and his supplications and prostrations will not be beneficial to him, but he will become guilty before God as well as before His angels. (Here) ends the regulations for ministers and their associates. **[35]**

---

[24] That is, to make up the 75.

ܚܙܘ ܟܠ ܡܥܡܕܝܢ ܒܗܕܐ ܕܦܬܓܡܐ ܐܠܗܘܬܗ ܒܪܘܓܐ ܕܡܫܡܫܢܐ ܠܐܣܝܐ ܐܝܬ
ܒܠܒܗܘܢ. ܦܠܟ ܗܘܝܐ ܢܣܓܘܕ ܡܥܢܝܢ ܕܫܝܠܬܐ ܘܢܥܒܕܘܢ ܘܢܒܥܐ ܡܘܥܒܐ ܠܗ
ܘܠܡܙܒܢܘܬܐ ܡܡܝܬܢܘܬܐ ܡܥܢܝܢ ܕܫܝܠܬܐ.
ܘܐܢ ܐܝܟ ܕܐܡܪ ܕܐܢ ܡܪܝ ܗܘ ܠܐܣܝܐ ܡܥܢܝܢ: ܡܬܠܡܝܕܐ ܐܘܦܝ ܐܡܪܘܢ
ܡܡܢ ܐܢܬܘܢܬܐ ܒܝܘܡܐ. ܘܐܡܪܝܢ ܕܐܢ[25] ܗܘ ܡܢܐ ܕܐܬܦܢܝ ܢܡܠܠ ܡܢܐ ܗܘ̈ܐ
ܠܝ ܡܬܐܪܢܐ ܐܠܐ ܐܘܦܝܢ ܣܝܡ ܒܒܪܐ ܗܘܐ ܠܝ ܡܬܐܪܢܐ.
ܘܐܘܦ ܡܕܪܪܐ ܐܢܫܐ ܡܢ ܐܘܪܫܠܡ ܡܦܩܐ ܐܢ ܓܒܪ ܐ̄ܠܡܥܡܕ ܠܒܢܝܢܐ
ܡ̈ܫܠܡܢܘܬܗ ܢܥܒܕܘܢ ܐܦ* ܠܗܘܢ ܐܒܘܗܝ ܗܘ ܕܒܫܡܝܐ. ܐܢ ܕܝܢ ܠܐ ܐ̄ܠܡܥܡܕ
ܠܒܢܝܢܐ ܡܫܠܡܢܘܬܗ ܐܦܠܐ ܐܒܘܗܝ ܢܥܒܕܘܢ ܠܗܘܢ ܡܫܠܡܢܘܬܗ. ܗܘܝ
ܒܗܕܐ ܕܐܡܪ ܡܫܠܡܢܘܬܐ ܘܠܐ ܡܫܠܡܢܘܬܐ ܚܙܘ ܟܠ ܒܪܢܫܐ ܕܦܠܟ ܗܘܝܐ ܢܥܒܕܘܢ
ܡܥܢܝܢ ܕܫܝܠܬܐ.
ܘܗܟܝܠ ܢܒܥܐ ܡܘܥܒܐ ܡܥܢܝܢ ܕܫܠܬܐ. ܐܡܪ ܒܪ ܐܬܦܠܝܠ ܕܠܐܬܘ ܩܕܡ
ܐܠܗܐ. ܐܢ ܓܒܪ ܢܥܒܕܘܢ ܘܐܡܪ ܡܥܒܕܘܢ ܠܝ ܐܝܟ ܕܐܦ ܗܘ ܡܫܡܫ. ܗܘܐ
ܡܡܠܠܐ ܕܡܠܗ ܚܙܪ ܩܕܡ ܐܠܗܐ ܘܢܥܒܕܘܢ ܠܗ ܒܠܒܗܝܢ ܡܫܠܡܘܬܗ. ܐܝܟܢ
ܠܐ ܡܫܡܫ ܘܐܡܪ ܡܥܒܕܘܢ ܠܝ ܐܝܟ ܕܐܦ ܗܘ ܡܫܡܫܢ ܗܘܐ ܡܡܠܠܐ ܕܡܠܗ
ܕܒܠܒܘܬܐ ܩܕܡ ܐܠܗܐ. ܘܠܗܘܢ ܕܠܐ ܢܥܒܕܘܢ ܠܗ ܠܒܢܘܗܝ ܐܠܐ ܪܘܓܙܐ ܢܦܠܐ ܠܗ
ܡܢ ܐܠܗܐ ܟܠ ܕܕܓܠ ܡ̈ܫܡܗܘܢ. ܘܒܠܒܘܬܗ ܠܗܘܐ ܣܛܢܐ ܘܠܐ ܡ̈ܫܬܩܝ ܠܗ
ܒܝ̈ܬܐ ܘܡܬܓܒܪܬܐ ܐܠܐ ܗܘܐ ܡܡܪܚܐ ܩܕܡ ܐܠܗܐ ܘܩܕܡ ܡ̈ܫܠܡܘܗܝ. ܡܫܡܫ
ܠܐܣܝܐ ܕܐܝܬ ܟܠ ܡܫܡܫܢܐ ܘܟܠ ܢܦܫܗܘܢ܀*

[25]Ms ܕܐܢ

17. *Regulations on prayers and prostrations (segdotho) and their number (required) for the Patriarchs and their associates, (i.e.), Maphrians, Metropolitans, bishops, and presbyters:*

These five orders do not have specified times for prayers, and no special regulations for prostrations. But they shall continuously remain in fasting, prayers and prostrations (*segdotho*) because the souls of men have been entrusted to them, i.e., the sheepfold of Christ. They shall be vigilant and diligent in the shepherding of the rational and Christian sheep, night and day: they should be watchful for them, so that not a single one among them may perish. As shepherds, they shall take their staff in their hands, leading the flock from one pasture to another, and from one (source of) water to another, they do not take rest or sit night and day, except for two times (*'edone*). In heat and cold, they lead them to shelter.[26] Thus each of the (above) five orders ought to be vigilant and diligent night and day for the shepherding of Christ's flock without (specific) times or regulations.

(However), regulations and times have been appointed for slack shepherds: [**36**] if they are lazy and neglect continuous prayers, they shall perform ten specified (prayers) and 150 prostrations in the church by which the flock of Christ shall be refreshed. For the Psalms, hymns and canticles are nourishment for the rational flock, in specified times, and the rest of the hours there shall be rest for the flock, like heat or cold for sheep which are dumb animals. the flock of animals. Warmth is needed and necessary in this toilsome world, while cold is the slumber and natural drowsiness of the dark night. (This is) so that (the sheep) do not suffer a burden beyond their strength.

---

[26] The manuscript has *seṭro*, 'side'; conceivably the side of Christ (John 19:34), the source of the sacraments, is intended; but it seems more likely that this is a corruption of *setoro*, 'shelter, protection'. I am grateful to S. Brock for this comment.

17. ܬܘܒ ܠܨܘܡܐ ܕܒܥ̈ܘܬܐ ܘܡܫܬܘܬܐ ܕܒܗܘܢ ܘܡܥܡܘܠܗܘܢ ܕܦܛܪ̈ܝܗܘ ܡ̈ܦܩܢܐ
ܘܡܝܛܪ̈ܘܦܘܠܝܛܐ ܘܐܦܝܣܩܘܦܐ ܘܩܫܝ̈ܫܐ.
ܗܟܢ ܣܥܡܐ ܡܘܠܟܐ ܟܠܗ ܠܟܠܗܘܢ ܕܝܪ̈ܐ ܘܡܕܝܢ̈ܬܐ ܠܟܢܘ̈ܫܬܐ ܘܠܐ ܠܨܘܡܐ
ܒܥܕܐ ܠܥܕ̈ܬܐ. ܐܠܐ ܐܡܬܝ ܕܗܘܐ ܒܦܘܡܐ ܘܒܟܬܒܐ ܡܛܠ ܕܐܬܗܡܢܘ
ܢܦܩܬܐ ܕܚܫܝܐ ܐܘܟܝܬ ܡܢܚܬܐ ܕܡܫܝܚܐ: ܢܗܘܘܢ ܒܢܝܗ ܘܡܫܠܡܝܢ ܥܠ
ܙܒܢܐ ܕܚܕܐ ܡܟܬܒܢܐ. ܘܡܬܚܫܒܐ ܒܟܠܗ ܘܒܐܬܪܐ. ܘܐܢܫܘܢ ܗܘܐ ܠܗܘܢ ܒܗܘܢ
ܘܠܐ ܢܠܒܫ ܡܢܗܘܢ ܘܠܐ ܚܕ: ܐܡܬܝ ܕܫܒܬܐ ܢܦܩܝܢ ܡܫܡܫܢܘܗܝ ܒܬܪܝܗܘܢ
ܘܡܡܠܠܝܢ ܠܟܠܗ ܡܢ ܙܒܢܐ ܠܙܒܢܐ ܘܡܢܝܢܐ ܠܡܢܐ ܘܠܐ ܢܫܬܥܐ ܘܠܐ ܢܠܒܫ
ܟܠܗܘܢ ܘܒܐܢܫܐ ܡܛܠ ܡܢ ܒܬܪ ܚܕܐ. ܟܢܘ̈ܫܐ ܘܩܛܘܪ̈ܐ ܡܛܠܠܝܢ ܐܝܟ
ܠܡܛܪܐ[27]. ܗܟܢܐ ܐܝܟ ܠܒܝ[28] ܡܢ ܗܟܢ ܚܟܝܡܐ ܡܘܠܟܐ ܕܗܘܐ ܕܐܡܪ
ܘܡܫܡܠܝܢ ܟܠܗܘܢ ܘܒܐܢܫܐ ܥܠ ܙܒܢܐ ܕܥܠܡܐ ܡܫܝܚܝܬܐ ܕܠܐ ܒܕܒܚܐ ܘܠܐ
ܠܐܢܫܐ.
ܘܠܐܢܫܐ ܘܒܢܝܐ ܠܙܒܢܐ ܕܡܠܐ ܐܬܬܩܢܘ. ܕܐܢ ܢܬܩܢܘܢ* ܘܗܢܘܢ ܡܢ
ܐܢܫܐ ܕܥܠܡܐ ܟܕ ܡܬܚܫܒܐ ܘܟܠ ܡܥܕܬܐ ܕܒܢܝܐ ܢܬܩܢܘܢ ܕܐܬܟܢܫܘ
ܒܗܘܢ ܟܠܗܘܢ ܡܫܝܚܝܬܐ. ܡܛܠ ܕܡܕܡ ܘܡܢܝܢܐ ܘܠܦܘܩܕܢܐ ܠܦܘܪܫܢܐ
ܐܢܘܢ ܟܠܗܘܢ ܡܟܬܒܢܐ. ܟܕ ܗܘ ܡܬܚܫܒ ܘܡܫܪܐ ܕܒܢܝܐ ܢܬܚܫܒܐ ܠܗܘܐ ܟܠܗܘܢ
ܐܝܟ ܚܘܒܐ ܘܗܘܐ ܟܠܗܘܢ ܡܫܝܚܝܬܐ ܘܡܫܡܠܝܢ. ܘܚܘܒܐ ܐܢܘܢ ܠܟܝܢܐ
ܘܐܢܫܝܢܐ ܕܟܠܡܕܡ ܗܘ ܠܐܡܐ. ܘܗܘܐ ܐܢܘܢ ܡܢܗܘܢ ܘܡܫܡܠܝܢ ܚܝܠܐ
ܕܟܠܗ ܚܘܒܐ ܘܠܐ ܠܐܢܫ ܗܘܐ ܠܟܠܗ ܡܢ ܚܝܠܐ܀

[27] Probably ܡܛܪܐ.
[28] One would expect ܠܒܝܬ ܚܕ (Brock).

After that: those who pray should add (the number of) prayers in the church, (with prayers) in their cells or in another place. If they do not do so, there will be no grace for them in the presence of God. Because he does what is commanded to do. Again, "unless your righteousness exceeds that of the scribes and the Pharisees, you will not enter the kingdom of heaven" (Matt. 5:20, *Harklean*). That is, you will not become participants in the Good Tidings of the Gospel. But if the prayers and supplications exceed, they will become children of the Most High and heirs of the kingdom of heaven, forever and ever. Amen. [**37**]

18. *Introduction to the prayers and prostrations (segdotho) in them and their numbers for the Patriarchs and the five ranks with them*:

When the hour of the prayer comes, he shall stand up and shall come earnestly and diligently from his house or cell to the church and say on the road the following Psalm: "To You O Lord, I lift up my soul" (Ps. 25). As he enters the church, he shall say: "I have entered Your house, etc.". And he shall stand before the holy altar and purify himself from human thoughts and shall lift up his heart to the Holy Trinity and he should say: "Holy, Holy, Holy Lord Almighty, the heaven and earth are full of His glory; Hosanna in the highest". And he shall begin depicting the crucified Son before his eyes: "Holy art Thou O God; Holy art Thou O Almighty, Holy art Thou O Immortal, who was crucified for us have mercy upon us". He should make the sign of the cross upon himself and prostrate (*nesgud*). Again, "Holy art Thou O God (etc.)" and shall make the sign of the cross upon himself and kneel down (*nesgud*). And again "Holy art Thou O God" and shall make the sign of the cross upon himself and prostrate (*nesgud*). And then he shall say, "Lord, have mercy upon us; Lord have mercy upon us; Lord have pity [**38**] and mercy upon us; Glory to You, O Lord, Glory to You, O Lord; Glory to You, our hope forever."

ܘܒܬܪ ܗܠܝܢ ܡܕܒܪ̈ܢܐ ܢܛܪܘܢ ܙܕ̈ܩܬܐ ܕܥܕܬܐ ܒܩܘܕ̈ܫܝܬܐ ܐܘ ܠܥܝܕܐ ܕܗܘܬܐ
ܕܐܝܬ. ܐܢ ܠܐ ܢܛܪܘܢ ܠܡܫܡܫܘܬܐ ܠܐ ܢܗܘܐ ܠܗܘܢ ܩܕܡ ܐܠܗܐ. ܡܛܠ ܕܗܘ
ܕܐܬܦܣ ܠܡܫܡܫ ܥܡܗ. ܘܐܦ ܕܐܢ ܠܐ ܢܬܡܠܟܘܢ ܕܢܫܬܡܫܘܢ ܠܗܢ ܡܢ ܕܩܫ̈ܝܫܐ
ܘܩܫ̈ܝܫܐ ܠܐ ܬܐܟܠܘܢ ܠܡܫܡܫܘܬܐ ܕܡܫܝܚܐ. ܐܘܟܝܬ ܠܐ ܗܘܝܢ ܐܝܟܢ ܐܬܘ ܡܫܬܐܣܐ
ܒܡܕܝܢܬܐ ܐܘܪܫܠܡ. ܐܝܟ ܢܛܪܘܢ ܙܕ̈ܩܬܐ ܘܒܘܟܪ̈ܐ ܢܗܘܘܢ ܒܢ̈ܝܗܘܢ ܕܡܕܝܢܬܐ
ܘܡܢܘ̈ܬܐ ܕܡܠܟܘܬܐ ܡܫܝܚܝܬܐ ܠܟܠܗܘܢ ܒܢ̈ܝܢܫܐ ܐܢܫ ❖*

18. ܡܛܠ ܕܙܕ̈ܩܬܐ ܘܡܬܢ̈ܬܐ ܕܒܗܘܢ ܘܩܘܪ̈ܒܢܐ ܕܡܠܟܘܢ ܕܦܛܝ̈ܪܘܗܝ ܥܠܝܗ
ܡܢ ܗܠܝܢ ܚܫܚܐ ܡܘܬܪ̈ܬܐ:

ܐܡܪܝܢ ܕܗܘܐ ܚܕܐ ܕܙܟܘܬܐ ܡܫܬܠܡܢܘܬܐ ܘܢܦܩܘܬܗ ܢܦܩ ܘܐܬܐ ܡܢ ܒܝܬܐ ܐܘ
ܡܟܠܬܐ ܠܥܕܬܐ ܘܐܡܪ ܠܐܘܪܚܐ ܡܕܡ ܗܘܐ ؛ ܠܟܘܢ ܡܪܝܐ ܢܦܩ ܐܘܟܠܘ.
ܘܗܘ ܕܥܠܠ ܠܥܕܬܐ ܢܐܡܪ ܠܟܘܡܪܐ ܐܠܗܐ ܚܕܐ ܘܡܪܝܐ ܘܢܦܩ ܩܕܡ
ܡܕܒܚܐ ܩܕܝܫܐ ܘܢܕܥ ܢܦܫܗ ܡܢ ܣܘܥܪ̈ܢܐ ܐ̱ܢܫܐ ܘܢܦܩ ܠܟܘ ܠܫܠܡܘܬܐ
ܩܕܝܫܬܐ. ܘܐܡܪ ܩܕܝܫ ܩܕܝܫ ܩܕܝܫ ܡܪܝܐ ܚܝܠܬܢܐ ܕܡܠܝܢ ܫܡܝܐ ܘܐܪܥܐ
ܬܫܒܘܚܬܗ ܐܘܫܥܢܐ ܒܡܪ̈ܘܡܐ. ܘܢܐܡܪ ܟܕ ܙܩܦ ܠܒܪܐ ܩܕܡ ܚܬܢܘܗܝ ܟܕ ܙܩܝܦ
ܩܕܝܫ ܐܠܗܐ ܩܕܝܫ ܚܝܠܬܢܐ ܩܕܝܫ ܠܐ ܡܝܘܬܐ ܕܐܨܛܠܒܬ ܚܠܦܝܢ
ܘܐܬܪܚܡܥܠܝܢ. ܘܢܪܝܡ ܐܝܕܗ ܥܠ ܐܦ̈ܘܗܝ ܘܢܨܠܐ. ܘܐܘܦ ܩܕܝܫ
ܐܠܗܐ ܘܢܪܝܡ ܐܝܕܗ ܥܠ ܐܦ̈ܘܗܝ ܘܢܨܠܐ. ܘܐܘܦ ܩܕܝܫ ܐܠܗܐ.
ܘܢܪܝܡ ܐܝܕܗ ܘܢܨܠܐ ܘܢܐܡܪ ܡܪܝ ܐܬܪܚܡܥܠܝܢ. ܡܪܝ ܐܬܪܚܡܥܠܝܢ. ܡܪܝ
ܐܬܪܚܡܥܠܝܢ. ܡܪܝ ܚܘܣ* ܘܪܚܡܥܠܝܢ. ܫܘܒܚ ܠܟ ܡܪܝ. ܫܘܒܚܠܟ ܡܪܝ.
ܫܘܒܚ ܠܟ ܡܪܢ ܠܥܠܡ.

By three sanctifications of the Trinity, he should sanctify his soul, and with three sanctifications of the Son, he should sanctify his body and stand erect stretching out his hands and raising his eyes above towards the Father and say: "Our Father who art in heaven".

Then the usual *Shubḥo* ('Glory')[29] and the Psalm "Have mercy upon me, O God" (Ps. 51) and he shall make six prostrations (*segdotho*) and he shall be blessed by [kissing] the Holy Gospel or by the door of the sanctuary and (then) stand in his place.

Again the appropriate *Shubḥo* ('Glory') and the *'enyono, sedro, qole*, etc., until the prayer is concluded. Then he should say with the whole congregation "Holy art Thou O God... Who was crucified for us, have mercy upon us", and shall make the sign of the cross upon himself and prostrate (*nesgud*). Again, "Holy art Thou O God", and make the sign of the cross upon himself and prostrate (*nesgud*). And again, "Holy art Thou O God" and make the sign of the cross and prostrate (*nesgud*). (Then) "Lord have mercy upon us, etc." as it is written above and he should say these, "Lord have mercy upon us" three times with three prostrations (*segdotho*) and then he should stand erect and say, "Our Father who art in heaven" as above, and the prayer is completed with eighteen **[39]** prostrations. Thus the five prayers of the day should be completed: *Ramsho, Sapro*, Third, Sixth, and Ninth hour, totaling 90 prostrations (*segdotho*), with 21 in *Sutoro*, 39 in *Lilyo*, making a total of 150.

---

[29] That is, the initial Trinitarian doxology, "Glory to the Father and the to the Son and to the Holy Spirit".

ܒܠܒܠܬܐ ܡܩܘܡܐ ܕܠܒܪܐ ܢܦܩܐ ܢܦܫܗ ܘܒܠܒܠܬܐ ܡܩܘܡܐ ܕܐܬܒܠܒܠܘܬܐ ܢܦܩܐ
ܦܓܪܗ. ܘܢܗܘܐ ܬܘܕܝܬܐ ܡܢ ܦܬܟܪܐ ܐܒܘܗܝ ܘܡܬܢܫܡ ܒܢܘܗܝ ܠܟܠ
ܠܗܘܐ ܐܒܐ ܘܐܡܪ ܐܒܘܢ ܕܒܫܡܝܐ.
.ܘܒܠܘܥ ܡܘܒܠܐ ܕܚܝܢ ܘܡܬܥܣܘܪܐ ܕܡܫܒܚܝܢ ܠܐܠܗܐ ܘܡܘܕܝܢ ܠܗ ܩܠܐ
ܡܫܒܚܬܐ ܘܠܥܠܡ ܡܢ ܐܘܟܠܢܝ ܡܟܝܠ ܐܘ ܬܘܒܐ ܕܡܟܝܠܐ ܘܢܗܘܐ ܒܘܠܬܐ
ܕܡܠܟܗ ❖
ܘܬܘܒ ܡܘܒܠܐ ܕܚܝܢ ܘܚܝܠܐ ܘܫܘܪܐ ܘܟܠܐ ܘܡܪܟܐ ܒܝܕܐ ܕܡܫܬܡܠܝܢܘܬܐ
ܙܒܢܐ ܘܫܘܝܢ ܢܐܡܪ ܒܗܘ ܦܠܚܘ ܒܝܬܐ ܡܝܩܪ ܠܐܠܗܐ [ܡܪܝܐ]. ܕܐܬܓܠܝܬܗ
ܢܠܦܢ ܐܬܥܣܒܪܢ ܘܢܗܘܘܢ ܙܒܢܐ ܒܠܠ ܐܦܘܗܝ ܘܡܘܕܝܢ. ܘܬܘܒ
ܡܝܩܪ ܠܐܠܗܐ ܘܢܗܘܘܢ ܙܒܢܐ ܘܡܘܕܝܢ. ܘܬܘܒ ܡܝܩܪ ܠܐܠܗܐ ܘܢܗܘܘܢ
ܙܒܢܐ ܘܡܘܕܝܢ. ܡܢ ܐܬܥܣܒܪܢ ܘܡܪܟܐ ܐܝܟ ܕܒܟܠ ܥܠܡܐ ܘܐܡܪ
ܠܗܠܝܢ ܡܢ ܐܬܥܣܒܪܢ ܬܠܬ ܕܒܢܝ ܒܠܒܠ ܡܫܒܚܬܐ ܘܒܠܘܥ ܢܗܘܘܢ
ܡܢ ܬܘܒ ܘܐܡܪ ܐܒܘܢ ܕܒܫܡܝܐ ܐܝܟ ܡܩܕܫܬܐ ܘܡܫܬܡܠܝܢܘܬܐ ܙܒܢܬܗ
ܒܡܫܒܚܬܐ*ܐܬܥܣܒܪܢ. ܘܗܘܝܐ ܢܬܥܣܒܪܢ ܙܒܢܬܐ ܚܕܐ ܕܐܬܥܒܕܐ: ܘܕܘܟܪܢܐ
ܘܕܘܪܫܐ ܘܬܠܬ ܫܢܝܢ ܘܕܝܢܐ ܫܢܝ ܘܐܬܥܒܕܢ. ܒܢܝ ܬܩܢܝܢ ܡܫܒܚܬܐ
ܘܕܝܘܬܪܐ ܩܠܐ. ܘܕܠܚܝܐ ܠܟܘܢ ܗܘܝܢ ܒܠܗܘܢ ܩܡ.

Prostrations (*segdotho*) of *Sutoro*: Holy, Holy, Holy, etc., and he shall say, "Holy art Thou O God" three times with three prostrations (*segdotho*) as in the rest of the prayers and the appropriate *shubḥo* and the Psalm , "Have mercy upon me according to Your grace (Ps. 51)" with six prostrations (*segdotho*), and "Our Father who art in heaven" and again three prostrations (*segdotho*). Instead of the 'Christian prostrations' (*segdotho mshihoyotho*), he shall beseech for them mercies, compassion and forgiveness of sins, and he sings (*mshabah*) the praise of *Sutoro*, *sedro*, *qolo*, *bo'utho* and *takshaptho*. To conclude, they say two psalms, "He who sits in the shelter of the Most High" and "I shall lift up my eyes to the mountains" (Ps. 91 + 121), and with it he shall prostrate (*nesgud*) six times (*segdotho*).

Then "Blessed is the honour of the Lord from His place forever (Ex 3:1)", "Holy Trinity, have mercy upon us", and he should prostrate (*nesgud*). Again, "Blessed is the honour (of the Lord)" and prostrate. Again, "Lord, have mercy upon us, etc.". Then, "Our Father who art in heaven" and his prayer in full (has) 21 prostrations (*segdotho*). And again, "we believe in One (True) God". Thus ends the prayers of *Sutoro*.

Again, he shall say the prayers of *Lilyo* like the rest of the prayers: [**40**] "Holy, Holy, Holy, Lord Almighty, whose glory fills heaven and earth, Hosanna in the Highest. Blessed is He who came and is coming in the name of the Lord. Hosanna in the Highest". And (then) he should begin, "Holy art Thou O God", three times, with three prostrations (*segdotho*). And again, "Lord, have mercy upon me, etc.". Standing erect and raising his eyes up above upwards towards the Father, he should say, "Our Father, who art in heaven", followed by three prostrations (*segdotho*).

ܬܫܒܚܬܐ ܕܣܪ̈ܦܐ: ܩܕܝܫ ܩܕܝܫ ܩܕܝܫ ܘܒܥܢ̈ܢܐ ܘܐܡܪ. ܩܕܝܫܬ ܠܐܠܗܐ ܐܟܠ
ܪ̈ܩܝܥܐ ܒܫܠܡܐ ܬܫܒܚܬܐ ܐܝܟ ܥܢ̈ܢܐ ܕܪ̈ܥܡܬܐ. ܘܡܩܒܠ ܕܟܠܗܘܢ ܘܡܕܡܘܪܐ
ܕܡܫܒܚܝܢ ܐܝܟ ܕܫܘܠܛܢ ܒܫܡܝܐ ܬܫܒܚܬܐ ܘܐܝܟ ܕܒܫܡܝܐ. ܘܐܘܟ ܠܟܠܐ
ܬܫܒܚܬܐ. ܚܠܦ ܬܫܒܚܬܐ ܡܫܒܚܢܝܬܐ ܘܢܒܥܐ ܠܗܘܢ ܕܡܝܐ ܘܡܘܡܝܐ ܘܫܘܒܚܐ
ܕܢܗܪ̈ܐ. ܘܡܫܡܫܝܢ ܫܘܟ ܕܫܘܠܛܐ. ܘܫܡܝܐ ܘܡܠܐ ܘܡܕܘܬܐ ܘܐܫܬܡܥܬܐ. ܘܡܢ
ܡܫܡܫܢܝܢ ܐܡܪܝܢ ܠܬܡܢ ܡܕܡܘܪܐ ܢܦܩ ܒܫܠܛܢܘܗ ܕܡܪܝܡܐ. ܘܐܪܡܝ ܒܢܝ̈
ܠܓܘܪܐ ܘܫܒܚܘ ܒܗ ܫܡ ܬܫܒܚܬܐ.
ܘܒܬܪܟܢ ܡܒܪܝܢ ܗܘ ܐܡܪܗ ܕܡܪܝܐ ܡܢ ܐܬܪܗ ܒܒܠܡ. ܠܐܠܗܘܬܐ ܩܕܝܫܬܐ
ܐܬܪܡܫܢܝܢ ܘܢܫܒܚܘܢ. ܘܐܘܟ ܡܒܪܝܢ ܗܘ ܐܡܪܗ ܘܢܫܒܚܘܢ ܘܐܘܟ ܡܢ
ܐܬܪܡܫܢܝܢ ܘܡܪܝܐ. ܘܐܘܟ ܐܟܘܢ ܕܒܫܡܝܐ. ܘܡܫܬܡܫܢܐ ܕܟܠܗ ܟܠ
ܬܫܒܚܬܐ ܘܐܘܟ ܡܫܡܫܝܢ ܒܫܢ ܠܐܠܗܐ ܀ ܡܠܫܢܐ ܕܟܠܬܐ ܕܫܘܠܛܐ܀
ܠܐܘܟ ܕܟܠܬܐ ܕܠܠܗܐ ܐܝܟ ܥܢ̈ܢܐ ܕܪ̈ܥܡܬܐ ܢܐܡܪ* ܩܕܝܫ ܩܕܝܫ ܩܕܝܫ ܡܪܝܐ
ܚܝܠܬܢܐ ܕܡܠܝܢ ܫܡܝܐ ܘܐܪܥܐ ܠܬܫܒܚܬܗ ܐܝܩܪܐ ܒܡܪ̈ܝܡܐ. ܒܪܝܟ ܕܐܬܐ
ܐܬܐ ܒܫܡܗ ܕܡܪܝܐ ܐܘܫܥܢܐ ܒܡܪ̈ܝܡܐ ܘܫܠܡܐ ܩܕܝܫܬ ܠܐܠܗܐ ܠܐܠܗܐ ܕܒܫܡܝܐ
ܒܠܠܟ ܬܫܒܚܬܐ. ܘܐܘܟ ܡܢ ܐܬܪܡܫܢܝܢ ܘܡܪܝܐ. ܘܫܡܥܡ ܡܢ ܠܐܪܥ
ܘܡܬܢܝܢ ܢܚܢ ܠܟܠܠ ܠܗܠ ܐܬܠ ܘܢܐܡܪ ܐܟܘܢ ܕܒܫܡܝܐ. ܘܒܬܪܗ ܠܐܟܠ
ܬܫܒܚܬܐ.

And the *shubḥo* of the *Lilyo* and "Have mercy upon me O God" (Ps. 51) with six prostrations (*segdotho*) and he should say this prayer: "My Lord and My God Jesus Christ, I offer prostrations (*segdotho*) before Your Magnificence and of Your Father and of Your Holy Spirit for the flock purchased with Your precious blood, that it may be delivered from all the workings of the enemy". Or let him beseech mercies and absolution for the sheepfold of Christ, (in another way) as he knows. He should not be blessed by the Gospel, or by the door of the sanctuary, nor by a bishop who is present except for the prostrations (*segdotho*) towards the sanctuary, and the bishop, for in the *lilyo* there is no need for kissing.

When the first nocturn (*'edono*) is held, he shall say, "Blessed is the honour of the Lord from His place forever (Ez. 3:12)", "Holy Trinity, have mercy upon us" and prostrate (*nesgud*). "Lord, have mercy upon us, **[41]** Lord, have pity on my sinfulness and upon the whole sheepfold" and prostrate (*nesgud*). And again, "Blessed is the honour of the Lord from His place forever, Holy Trinity, have mercy upon us", and prostrate. And, "Lord, have mercy upon us, Lord, have pity on my sinfulness and upon Your entire sheepfold", and kneel down. "Lord, have mercy upon us; Lord, have mercy upon us; Lord, have mercy upon us; Lord, answer us and have mercy upon us. Glory to You, O Lord; Glory to You, O Lord; Glory to You our hope forever" and he shall say, "Our Father who art in Heaven", making six prostrations (*segdotho*) between two nocturns (*'edone*) that are counted, (that is) three prostrations at the end of the first nocturn and three prostrations at the end of the second nocturn. Thus second *'edono* should be completed.

ܘܫܘܒܚܐ ܕܟܠܗ ܘܪܫܡ ܒܢܝ ܐܠܗܐ ܒܩ̈ܠܐ ܥ̈ܢܝܬܐ ܘܐܡܪ ܙܡܪܬܐ ܗܕܐ: ܡܪܝ
ܘܐܠܗܘܢ ܡܫܘܢ ܡܫܒܚܐ ܥ̈ܢܝܬܐ ܡܩܪܒ ܐܢܐ ܩܕܡ ܕܟܠܗ ܘܐܒܘܗܝ ܘܪܘܚܗ
ܩܕܝܫܐ ܣܠܩ ܟ̈ܢܐ ܪܚܡܬܐ ܒܕܡܘܬ ܡܫܪܐ ܕܐܬܦܪܐ ܡܢ ܦܠܚܘܢ ܡܫܡܫܢܘܬܗ ܕܗܘ
ܕܫܘܟܠܐ. ܐܘ ܢܟܝܐ ܬܡܝܗܐ ܘܫܘܦܪܐ ܠܡܪܚܡܢܘܬܐ ܡܫܝܚܝܬܐ ܐܒܘܢ ܕܢܦܩ. ܘܠܐ
ܢܬܒܪܝ ܡܢ ܐܘܣܝܗ ܘܠܐ ܡܢ ܬܘܪܐ ܕܡܕܒܪܐ ܘܠܐ ܡܢ ܣܘܥܐ ܕܡܐܢ. ܐܠܐ
ܥ̈ܢܝܬܐ ܠܡܕܒܪܢܐ ܘܡܫܡܫܢܐ ܡܛܠ ܕܟܠܗ ܠܐ ܫܘܐ ܥܠ ܢܬܡܠܠ.
ܘܟܕ ܡܫܬܡܠܐ ܒܝܬ ܩܕܝܫܐ: ܢܐܡܪ: ܡܒܪܟ ܗܘ ܐܝܩܪܗ ܕܡܪܝܐ ܡܢ ܐܬܪܗ
ܠܥܠܡ. ܐܠܗܘܬܐ ܩܕܝܫܬܐ ܐܬܪܚܡܥܠܝܢ: ܘܥܢܝܢ: ܡܪܝ
ܐܬܪܚܡܥܠܝܢ.ܡܪܝ ܚܘܣ ܥܠ ܣܗ̈ܕܘܬܐ ܘܥܠ ܦܠܚܐ ܡܪܚܡܢܝ. ܘܥܢܝܢ.
ܘܬܘܒ ܡܒܪܟ ܗܘ ܐܝܩܪܗ ܕܡܪܝܐ ܡܢ ܐܬܪܗ ܠܥܠܡ. ܐܠܗܘܬܐ ܩܕܝܫܬܐ
ܐܬܪܚܡܥܠܝܢ. ܘܥܢܝܢ ܘܡܪܝ ܐܬܪܚܡܥܠܝܢ.* ܡܪܝ ܚܘܣ ܥܠ ܣܗ̈ܕܘܬܐ
ܘܥܠ ܦܠܚܐ ܡܪܚܡܢܝ ܘܥܢܝܢ. ܡܪܝ ܐܬܪܚܡܥܠܝܢ. ܡܪܝ ܐܬܪܚܡܥܠܝܢ.
ܡܪܝ ܐܬܪܚܡܥܠܝܢ. ܡܪܝ ܚܘܣ ܘܐܬܪܚܡܥܠܝܢ. ܫܘܒܚܐ ܠܟ ܡܪܝ. ܫܘܒܚܐ ܠܟ
ܡܪܝ. ܫܘܒܚܐ ܠܟ ܒܪܝ ܠܥܠܡ ܘܢܐܡܪ ܐܒܘܢ ܕܒܫܡܝܐ. ܗܦܟܝܢ ܫܡܥ
ܥ̈ܢܝܬܐ ܥܡܗ ܕܒܝܬܐ ܠܒܝܬܐ ܡܬܢܩ̈ܦܝܢ ܐܠܐ ܥ̈ܢܝܬܐ ܠܫܘܠܡ ܕܒܝܬܐ ܩܕܡܝܐ
ܘܬܠܬܐ ܥ̈ܢܝܬܐ. ܠܫܘܠܡ ܕܒܝܬܐ ܬܪܝܢܐ ܢܬܚܬܡܢ ܕܒܝܬܐ ܕܬܪܝܢ.

Again he shall say as we have specified, "Blessed is the honour of the Lord from His place forever, Holy Trinity, have mercy upon us" and prostrate. Again, "Blessed is the honour of the Lord, etc.", and prostrate. "Lord, have mercy upon us", and prostrate. "Lord, have mercy upon us" as usual and say "Our Father who art in heaven", making six prostrations between two nocturns. When the third nocturn is celebrated, it shall be done as follows: "Blessed is the honour of the Lord, etc.", with six prostrations (*segdotho*) and "Our Father who art in heaven". When the fourth nocturn is celebrated, he shall say, "Glory to God in the Highest [**42**] in full and prostrate (*nesgud*) six times in it.

And again, "Holy art Thou O God, Holy art Thou Almighty, Holy art Thou Immortal, who was crucified for us have mercy upon us", and prostrate. Again, "Holy art Thou O God, etc.", and prostrate. And again, "Holy art Thou O God" and prostrate. "Lord, have mercy upon us, etc." as usual. And "Our Father who art in heaven" and the prayer of *Lilyo* should be completed with 36 prostrations. These all together make in a day (*yaumo*), (that is) night and daytime (*imomo*) 150 prostrations. The patriarchs and his associates ought to complete these ten prayers and 150 prostrations (*segdotho*) in the church.

Those who have put on monastic garment, and are neither priests nor deacons, should follow this regulation. For those who have put on and clothed the garment of the clergy ought to be steadfast in prayers and prostrations (*segdotho*) like them (that is the higher clergy). If it happens that one among the Patriarchs or his associates, on account of worldly necessity, are prevented from coming to the church, he should pray wherever he is, in (his) cell, or in a house, or on a journey. And if there is no place to prostrate, because of worldly sense of pride, he should pray and prostrate (*nesgud*) in his soul, that is in his heart and God will count it [**43**] as complete. If there is no place for prayer, he should leave it till another time and (then) pray, so that the prayer is not entirely omitted – otherwise he will be required to repay ten thousand talents (*kakre*) when he has nothing at all (available) to repay.

ܢܐܡܪ ܬܘܒ ܐܟܡܐ ܕܐܡܪܢܢ. ܡܒܝܢ ܗ̄ܘ ܐܡܪܗ ܕܡܪܝܐ ܡܢ ܐܬܪܗ ܠܥܠܡ. ܬܫܒܘܚܬܐ ܩܕܝܫܬܐ ܐܬܘܣܦܬܘܢ ܘܫܘܚܠܦܗ. ܘܬܘܒ ܡܒܝܢ ܗ̄ܘ ܐܡܪܗ ܕܡܪܝܐ ܘܦܓܪܐ ܘܫܘܚܠܦܗ. ܘܡܢ ܐܬܘܣܦܬܘܢ ܘܫܘܚܠܦܗ. ܘܡܢ ܐܬܘܣܦܬܘܢ ܐܝܟ ܕܒܪܐ ܘܢܐܡܪ ܐܟܘܬ ܕܒܡܫܡܫܐ. ܗܕܐ ܗܝ ܩܕܝܫܬܐ ܒܡܠܬ ܕܒܪܐ ܠܕܒܪܐ. ܗܘ ܕܢܬܚܫܒ ܕܒܪܐ ܠܬܫܒܘܚܬܐ ܗܘܝܐ ܢܩܒ ܡܒܝܢ ܗ̄ܘ ܐܡܪܗ ܕܡܪܝܐ ܘܦܓܪܐ ܒܡܠܬ ܩܕܝܫܬܐ ܘܐܟܘܬ ܕܒܡܫܡܫܐ. ܗܘ ܢܬܚܫܒ ܕܒܪܐ ܕܩܒܠܬ ܢܐܡܪ ܠܬܫܒܘܚܬܐ ܠܐܠܗܐ ܒܡܪܘܡܐ*. ܡܫܡܫܢܝܬܐ. ܘܫܘܚܠܦܗ ܒܗ̇ ܡܠܬ ܩܕܝܫܬܐ. ܘܬܘܒ ܩܕܝܫܐ ܐܠܗܐ. ܩܕܝܫܐ ܚܝܠܬܢܐ. ܩܕܝܫܐ ܠܐ ܡܝܘܬܐ. ܕܐܨܛܠܒܬ ܚܠܦܝܢ ܐܬܘܣܦܬܘܢ. ܘܫܘܚܠܦܗ. ܘܬܘܒ ܩܕܝܫܐ ܐܠܗܐ ܘܦܓܪܐ ܘܫܘܚܠܦܗ. ܘܬܘܒ ܩܕܝܫܐ ܐܠܗܐ ܘܫܘܚܠܦܗ. ܡܢ ܐܬܘܣܦܬܘܢ ܐܝܟ ܕܒܪܐ. ܘܐܟܘܬ ܕܒܡܫܡܫܐ ܘܡܫܡܫܢܐ ܕܢܟܠܬܐ ܕܠܐܠܗܐ ܒܟܠܗ ܩܕܝܫܬܐ. ܒܝܕ ܦܠܓܘܬ ܚܕ ܡܘܡܐ ܠܐܠܗܐ ܘܐܡܝܢܐ ܩܡ ܩܕܝܫܬܐ. ܗܟܢ ܒܗܕ ܕܟܠܬܐ ܘܡܠܐ ܚܝܡܢ ܩܕܝܫܬܐ ܕܝܢ ܠܦܠܓܘܬܗ ܘܢܘܦܩܗܘܢ ܕܒܪܐ ܢܬܟܬܒܘܢ ܐܢܬܘܢ.

ܘܗܘܝ ܕܟܬܒܘ ܐܝܟܢܐ ܕܕܪܘܬܐ ܘܠܐ ܐܬܟܪܗܘܢ ܒܗܘܢ ܘܠܐ ܡܫܡܫܢܐ: ܗܢܐ ܠܐܘܡܢܐ ܐܝܟ ܒܟܠܗܘܢ. ܡܛܠ ܕܟܬܒܘ ܘܐܬܟܬܒܘ ܠܟܘܢܐ ܕܡܫܘܚܬܐ ܕܝܢ ܘܐܘܟܠܘܣܘܢ ܢܬܐܡܢ ܒܪܟܬܐ ܘܒܩܕܝܫܬܐ. ܐܝܟ ܕܝܢ ܠܟܢ ܡܢ ܦܠܓܘܬܗ ܐܘ ܡܢ ܢܦܘܩܗܘܢ ܡܛܠ ܐܝܟܢܐ ܕܟܬܒܐ ܗܢܐ ܠܘܩܒܠ ܘܠܐ ܢܬܬ ܠܒܪܬܐ: ܕܠܐ ܐܡܬܝ ܕܐܬܟܢܫ ܒܟܠܗܝܢ ܒܟܢܘܫܐ. ܐܦ ܟܠܗ ܐܬܪܐ ܠܡܫܡܫܢ ܡܛܠ ܗܘܢܪܐ ܕܟܬܒܐ ܕܠܐ ܘܫܘܚܠܦܗ ܒܢܦܫܗ ܐܘܟܠ ܒܟܠܗ. ܘܐܟܘܬ ܚܡܘܕ ܠܗ* ܡܫܡܫܢܘܬܐ. ܐܦ ܟܠܗ ܐܬܪܐ ܠܟܬܒܬܐ ܢܚܘܡ ܠܟܬܒܐ ܐܝܢܐ ܕܠܐ ܘܠܐ ܠܐܬܟܢܫ ܟܬܒܐ ܗܘ ܘܠܐ ܢܬܐܡܢ ܡܢܗ ܙܒܢ ܩ̈ܕܡܝܐ ܐܝܟܢ ܕܟܠܗ ܗܘ ܡܢܝܢ ܠܡܫܪܐ.

If they do not fulfill what we have said, the 18 prostrations, that they should make at the time of the *Qurobo*, will accuse them, making known and teaching them, that each (time) has 18 prostrations.

19. *Explanation of the prostrations (segdotho) during the [celebration] of the Holy Mysteries*:

First he (the celebrant) makes one prostration (*segdtho*),[30] stands up and holds the paten and the chalice, raises (them) and says, "I will exalt You my Lord King (Ps. 145:1)"; (then), "Holy art Thou O God", three times, and prostrates (*soged*) three (times),[31] and says, "Holy Trinity, have mercy upon us" and prostrates (*soged*) the fifth time.[32] And before taking the *gmurtho*[33] from the chalice, he prostrates (*soged*) a sixth time.[34]

When he dismisses (*kad mag'el*) and concludes saying, "I have entered Your house, etc.", and prostrates (*soged*) three times,[35] making nine (in total); and there are also the inclinations (*ghonotho*) which are also nine, making (in total) of eighteen. When the priest offers alone, he prostrates (*soged*) another 18 times; when he raises up the Mysteries, he takes the censor and prostrates (*soged*) three times before the altar to the left three times and to the right three times, and when he says, "We believe [**44**] in One God", again he prostrates (*soged*) nine times, making (a total) 18 times.

---

[30] In the preparation rites.

[31] Apparently the author refers to the prostrations during the opening Trisagion of the Pre-anaphora. However, the commentaries or the rubrics do not mention such a prostration.

[32] After the Creed, the celebrant prostrates (kneels down) before the altar and recites this prayer.

[33] Particle of the Eucharist.

[34] Prostration before communion.

[35] In post-communion.

ܘܐܦ ܠܐ ܢܫܬܡܥܘܢ ܠܗܠܝܢ ܕܐܡܪܝܢ ܣܦܪ̈ܝܬܐ ܐܪܡܝ̈ܬܐ ܕܣܦܪܝܢ ܒܟܪܝܐ ܕܡܘܪܒܐ
ܡܟܬܒ ܠܗܘܢ ܘܡܬܠܦ ܠܗܘܢ ܘܡܫܘܕܥ ܠܗܘܢ ܕܐܝܬ ܒܟܠ ܚܕܐ ܙܢܬܐ
ܐܪܡܝ̈ܬܐ ܣܦܪ̈ܝܬܐ܀

19. ܢܘܗܪܐ ܕܣܦܪ̈ܝܬܐ ܕܟܠܗܝܢ ܙ̈ܘܙܐ ܡܢܝ̈ܢܐ:

ܡܢܝܢܐ ܗ̇ܟܢ ܣܦܪܬܐ ܚܕܐ ܘܬܪܬܝܢ ܘܬܠܬ ܥܠܐ ܘܟܫܐ ܘܡܟܠܐ ܟܕ ܐܡܪ: ܐܘܪܡܣ ܡܪܢ ܡܠܟܐ. ܡܢܝܢܐ ܐܠܗܐ ܐܬܠܬ ܕܫܢܐ ܗܟܢ ܐܠܦܐ. ܘܟܕ ܐܡܪ ܐܠܦܘܬܐ ܡܢܝܢܬܐ ܐܬܘܣܦ ܠܟܠܗ. ܘܗܟܢ ܣܥܘܢܝܬܐ. ܘܡܢܗ ܕܡܬܠ ܠܡܘܪܬܐ ܡܢ ܒܬܐ ܗܟܢ ܗܠܬܠܬܐ.

ܘܟܕ ܡܟܠܠ ܘܡܫܬܡܠܐ ܐܡܪ: ܠܟܠܗܘܢ ܒܠܠ ܘܡܪܢܐ. ܐܠܦܐ ܕܪܒܘܬܐ ܗܟܢ ܐܠܦܐ. ܗܘܝܢ ܐܠܦ̈ܐ ܡܫܘܚܬܐ[36] ܐܠܦܝܢ. ܘܐܦ ܐܠܦ̈ܐ ܗܘܝܢ ܐܪܡܝ̈ܬܐ.
ܘܐܠܦܝܢ ܕܒܗܝܢ ܠܡܫܘܚܘܬܐ ܡܬܚܙܝܢ ܐ̱ܬ̈ܘܬܐ ܐܪܡܝ̈ܬܐ ܗ̇ܟܢ. ܐܠܦܝܢ ܕܡܢܝܢܐ ܠܐ̈ܘܪܐ ܦܫܠ ܠܡܦܪܢܐ ܘܗܟܢ ܡܢܗ ܡܕܒܪܐ ܐܠܦܐ. ܘܡܢ ܦ̈ܬܓܡܐ ܐܠܦܐ. ܘܡܢ ܡ̈ܫܡܥܬܐ ܐܠܦܐ. ܘܟܕ ܐܡܪ ܡܫܡܫܝܢ* ܟܝܢ ܐܠܗܐ ܗܘܝܐ ܠܐܘܒ ܗ̇ܟܢ ܐܠܦܐ ܐܚܪܢܝܬܐ.

[36] Ms ܐܬ̈ܘܬܐ.

Signs of the crosses over the Body and Blood are 18 (in number) and the crosses over the people are also 18. When the priest says "Love of God the Father", he makes (the sign of) the cross over his face and it is reckoned for himself; (then) one to the north and one to the south, and three towards the west, making (a total of) five. When he says, "May the mercies of God", five (signs of the) cross; and when he says, "May the grace of the Holy Trinity", another five (signs of the cross). When he dismisses (*mag'el*), three crosses, making a total 18 crosses. All these testify and confirm that in every prayer, there are 18 signs of the cross and[37] bowing downs (*segdotho*).

20. [*On the Lord's Prayer*]:

If these are not sufficent for you and slothfulness reigns over you, the prayer, "Our Father who art in heaven" will confirm for you and make you to grow in knowledge, because in it, there are ten verses and you say each prayer (in it) two times, in the beginning and at the end. The first word is the invocation of the Father and the nine others are supplications. There are 18 supplications (when it is said) two times. You ought to offer nine prostrations (*segdotho*) in the beginning of the prayer [**45**] and then you may dare to address the Father in nine supplications. At the end of the prayer, you should offer nine prostrations (*segdotho*), and address the Father in nine supplications. It is not right that supplication be offered without prostrations (*segdotho*). But first prostrations and then supplications. By these supplications, the prostrations are affirmed and the prayers may be accepted.

---

[37] Correcting *dsgdt'* to *wsgdt'* (Brock).

ܗܘܝܢ ܠܐܣܛܘܟܣܐ ܘܙܒ̈ܢܐ ܕܟܠ ܦܓܪܐ ܘܢܦܫܐ ܠܐܣܛܘܟܣܐ ܐܢܘܢ. ܘܙܒ̈ܢܐ ܕܟܠ ܥܠܡܐ ܠܐܣܛܘܟܣܐ ܠܐܘܟ ܐܢܘܢ. ܟܕܝܠ ܕܐܡܪ ܟܘܢܐ ܚܘܒܐ ܕܐܠܗܐ ܐܒܐ ܦܐܡ ܙܒܢܐ ܟܠ ܐܦܩܘܗܝ ܘܟܠܗ ܡܬܚܡܟ ܘܡܢ ܠܦܪܘܫܐ ܘܡܢ ܟܠܡܬܚܡܐ ܘܐܟܠܬܐ ܠܡܥܒܪܢܐ ܗܘܝܢ ܡ̈ܬܚܡܐ ܘܟܕܝܢ ܕܐܡܪ ܢܗܘܘܢ ܬ̈ܫܡܫܘܗܝ ܕܐܠܗܐ ܡܫ̈ܡܫܐ ܙܒ̈ܢܐ. ܘܡܢ ܐܡܪ: ܠܗܘܐ ܠܡܚܘܬܐ ܕܐܬܟܠܝܬܐ ܡܢܚܬܐ ܡܫܡܫܐ ܐܝܬܝܐ. ܘܡܢ ܡܫܟܠܠ ܠܟܠܬܐ ܙܒ̈ܢܐ ܟܢܘܢ ܠܐܣܛܘܟܣܐ ܙܒ̈ܢܐ ܦܠܚܝܢ ܦܠܚܗܘܢ ܦܗܘܪܝܢ ܘܡܣܬܪܝܢ ܕܟܠܠ ܙܒܢܬܐ ܐܝܟ ܠܐܣܛܘܟܣܐ ܙܒ̈ܢܐ ܘܡܫܡܠܝܬܐ[38]. ܘܐܦ ܗܟܝܠ ܠܐ ܡܫܡܫܝܢ ܟܝ ܘܡܫܟܢܫܢܘܬܐ ܡܫܟܠܠܐ ܟܠܝܗ:

20. ܙܒܢܬܐ ܕܐܝܟܢ ܕܡܫܡܫܐ ܡܫܪܝܐ ܠܗ ܘܡܫܘܫܠܐ ܠܗ ܡܢܟܠܬܐ. ܡܫܟܠܠ ܘܐܬܝܗ̇ ܟܠܗ̈ ܡܠܠܐ. ܘܟܦܠ ܡܢܐ ܙܒܢܬܐ ܠܬܐܡ ܕܟܬܝܒ ܐܡܪ ܐܝܟ ܟܢܗ̇ ܟܡܘܪܝܗ̇ ܘܟܘܠܗܘܢܗ̇. ܘܡܫܟܠܠܐ ܡܫܡܫܬܐ. ܡܢܝܬܐ ܕܐܬܐ ܐܝܬܝܗ̇ ܘܠܐܦܘ ܐܝܬܝܢܝܬܐ ܒܕ̈ܡܘܬܐ ܐܝܬܝܗܝܢ. ܠܬܐܡ ܕܦܫܝܬܐ ܠܐܣܛܘܟܣܐ ܟܕ̈ܡܘܬܐ ܐܝܬܝܗܝܢ. ܙܘܥ ܠܗ ܕܐܡܪܢ ܠܐܦܘ ܡܫܡܠܝܬܐ ܟܡܘܪܝ ܙܒܢܬܐ*ܘܟܠܘܪܝܢ ܕܐܦܪܝܣ ܕܐܡܪܐ ܠܟܠ ܟܠܐܦܘ ܒܕ̈ܡܘܬܐ. ܘܟܡܘܟܠܗ ܙܒܢܬܐ ܠܐܡܪܢ ܠܐܦܘ ܡܫܡܠܝܬܐ ܘܠܐܡܪܐ ܠܠܐܟܠ ܟܠܐܦܘ ܒܕ̈ܡܘܬܐ. ܘܠܐ ܙܘܥ ܕܟ̈ܘܬܐ ܢܬܐܡܪܢ ܘܠܐ ܡܫܡܠܝܬܐ ܐܠܐ ܡܫܡܫܐ ܡܫܡܠܝܬܐ ܘܟܠܘܪܝܢ ܟ̈ܘܬܐ. ܒܗܟܢ ܟ̈ܘܬܐ ܡܫܟܠܘܪܝܢ ܡܫܡܠܝܬܐ ܘܡܟܪ ܡܬܐܡܪܢ ܙܒ̈ܢܬܐ.

[38] Ms ܕܡܫܡܠܝܬܐ.

There is something further: the prayer of "Our Father who art in heaven" (is said) every day, night and day, 18 times: at *Ramsho* twice, at *Sutoro* twice, at *Lilyo* five times, at *Sapro* twice, third hour twice, sixth hour three times, one of them in *Qurobo* and ninth hour twice, making 18 times a day. This is enough for the instructed. If an argument is brought forth, we add the living and holy words which our Lord said in the venerable and life-giving Gospel, saying: "Therefore, the kingdom of heaven resembles a human king who wishes to settle accounts. One who owed ten thousand talents approached him, having no way to repay. His master ordered him to be sold (with) his wife and children and all that he had and to repay (Matt. 18:23–25). Who is [**46**] this man who owes such a huge amount, but one of the stewards of Christian faith who was entrusted with the souls of men? He is subject to the regulations and ecclesiastical laws, so he shall pray and prostrate (*nesgud*) for himself as well as for his flock.

21. *Interpretation*:

The Kingdom of God is the proclamation of the Gospel which resembles a king who is settling the accounts with his servants (Matt. 18:23). The one who owed him ten thousand talents is one of the stewards of the Gospel, who stands up day and night and is diligent for the members of his sheepfold, whether Patriarch, Maphrian or Metropolitan, bishop or priest, that is presbyter (*kashisho*), because the Gospel requires from each of them on the day of resurrection ten thousand talents, that is, fasting, prayers and prostrations (*segdotho*) prescribed for him apart from the additional ones he is going to offer.

ܘܐܦ ܐ̱ܢܫܐ ܡܕܡ ܙܟܘܬܐ ܕܐܟܘܬ ܕܟܡܟܡܐ ܦܠܐ ܡܘܡܐ: ܟܠܗ ܘܐܡܝܡܐ
ܠܐܣܛܘܟܣܐ ܕܟܝܢܐ. ܒܪܝܬܐ ܠܐܐܪ. ܘܟܣܝܘܬܐ ܠܐܐܪ ܘܟܠܗܝܢ ܡܢܗܘܢ ܕܟܝܢܐ.
ܘܥܦܪܐ ܠܐܐܪ. ܘܟܠܟܠ ܡܢܗ̇ ܠܐܐܪ. ܘܟܝܢܐ ܡܢܗ̇ ܠܟܠ. ܚܕܐ ܡܢܗܘܢ
ܒܡܘܪܐ ܘܟܠܡܬܩܢܢ ܠܐܐܪ ܕܟܝܢܐ ܗܘܝܢ ܠܐܣܛܘܟܣܐ ܡܘܫܐ ܒܡܘܡܐ:
ܗܟܢ ܠܒܪܘܬܐ ܗܩܡܢ. ܘܐܢ ܒܟܝܢܐ ܡ̈ܠܝܢ ܠܡܙ̈ܒܢܐ ܡ̈ܘܣܦܢ ܡܠܐ
ܚܝܠܐ ܘܡܬܝܡܢܐ ܕܐܡܪ ܡܪܝ ܒܐܘܓܠܝܘܢ ܗܟܢܐ ܘܡܣܝܒܐ ܒܗ ܐܡܪ:
ܡܬܒܗܪܐ ܐܠܘܗܝ ܡ̈ܠܟܘܬܐ ܕ̈ܫܡܝܐ ܠܒܪܢܫܐ ܡܠܟܐ ܗܘ ܕܥܒܕ ܠܡܥܡܕ
ܡܘܡܬܐ. ܐܬܡܪ ܠܗ ܚܕ ܡ̈ܢܝܢܐ ܕܬܟܘ ܒܟܪܐ. ܘܟܕ ܠܐ ܐܝܬ ܗ̱ܘܐ ܠܗ ܕܢܦ
ܡܕܡ ܠܡܦܪܥ ܦܩܕ ܡܪܗ ܕܢܙܒܢ ܗܘ ܘܐܢܬܬܗ ܘܒܢܘܗܝ ܘܟܠܡܕܡ ܕܐܝܬ
ܠܗ ܘܢܦܪܥ. ܡ̈ܢܘ* ܗܘܐ ܕܐܝܬ ܒܟܠܗܘܢ ܗܘܐ ܡܣܝܒܐ ܙܟܐ. ܐܠܐ ܚܕ ܡܢ ܙ̈ܟܝ
ܩ̈ܠܐ ܕܗܡܝܢܘܬܐ ܡܣܒܝܒܢܘܬܐ ܕܐܬܗܡܢ ܢܩ̈ܫܐ ܕܒܢܝܢܐ. ܘܟܠܐ ܠܐܝܟܢ
ܠܐܦ̈ܝܐ ܘܡܦ̈ܘܣܐ ܒܐܬܪܐ ܕܐܠܐ ܘܢܣܒܘܗܝ ܚܠܦ ܢܦܫܗ ܘܚܠܦ ܡܪܝܡܘܬܗ.

21. ܦܘܡܐ: ܡܬܒܗܪܐ ܕܡܫܝܐ ܐܡܝܢ ܗܒܪܐ ܐܘܟܝܬܐ ܕܐܬܡ̈ܢܝܢ
ܒܡܪܢܐ ܡܠܟܐ ܕܒܥܐ ܡܘܡܬܐ ܥܡ ܥ̈ܒܕܘܗܝ. ܗܘ ܕܚܝܒ ܙ̈ܟܘ ܥܣܪܐ ܐܠܦ̄
ܚܕ ܡܢ ܙ̈ܟܝ ܩ̈ܠܐ ܕܗܒܪܐ ܗܘ ܕܐܝܬ ܒܟܠܗ ܘܒܐܝܡܡܐ ܘܡܪܦ ܠܢܦܫܗ
ܘܠܒܢܝܐ ܕܡܪܝܡܘܬܗ. ܐܢ ܦܬܓܡܐ ܐܠܦ̄ ܐܘ ܡܦܪܫܐ ܐܘ ܡܬܪܘܦܘܬܐ ܐܘ̄
ܐܦܣܘܩܐ ܐܘ ܒܘܝܐ ܐܘܒܕܢ ܡܣܝܡܐ ܡܬܠܐ ܕܗܘ ܗܒܪܐ ܠܐܒܐ ܡܢ ܚܕ ܚܕ
ܡܢ ܗܟܢ ܒܡܘܡܐ ܕܡܣܟܢܬܐ ܙ̈ܟܘ ܥܣܪܐ ܐ̄ ܙܘܡܐ ܘܙܟ̈ܘܬܐ ܘܡܬܝ̈ܒܬܐ ܕܐܬܐܡܝܢ
ܒܟܠܗܘܢ ܡܬܠ ܡܢ ܠܒ̈ܬܐ ܕܠܐܝܢ ܕܢܦܪܥ.

If he is able to have fulfilled the regulations of fasting, prayers and prostrations, he will hear the pleasant and sweet voice, "Well done, good and faithful servant, you have been faithful over a little; I will set you over much (Matt. 25:23) that is, you have been faithful over the 'composite souls' (*naphshotho mrakbotho*) of human beings [**47**], I will set you upon the simple souls (*naphshoto phshiṭotho*) of angels,[39] "Enter into the joy of your Lord" (Matt. 25:21). If he will be found without fasting or not having observed the regulations on prayers and prostrations, he will hear that biter utterance saying, "Let him be sold, and let his wife, children and everything he has be sold to repay the ten thousand talents" (Matt. 18:25). When and how was this uncountable quantity come about for him? How much is the ten thousand talents ?

One *rebutho* (= ten thousand) is ten times a thousand. *Rebu* (pl. myriad) talent is one hundred thousand, making ten times one hundred, a thousand thousand, in total making one thousand times a thousand. A man has an obligation to (make) ten prayers and 150 prostrations a day. In ten days, 1500 (prostrations). Every month, it makes 4,500; making 54,750 a year. In ten years it will become 547,000. Five times four hundred thousand and seventy five thousand. (He probably counts 50 years) according to their number.

22. [*Prostrations during the recitation of Psalms*]

Again the (number of) prostrations each day in the Psalms of David is 150 that are to be completed and with them, [**48**] offences, transgressions, hateful things, blemishes and faults like them, and even more than them; from these an exceeding vast number will be assembled. And because of it the order went out to sell his wife, children and everything he had and to repay.

[39] 'Composite', i.e. joined to a body, and 'simple', not joined to a body.

ܐܝܟ ܕܐܡܪܢ ܕܡܫܬܟܚ ܠܐܣܘܬܐ ܕܢ̈ܦܫܐ ܘܦ̈ܓܪܐ ܘܡܫܬܪܝܬܐ ܕܡܫܚܢ ܒܪܐ ܗܠܐ
ܒܗܝܡܢܘܬܐ ܘܣܝܡܬܐ. ܡܛܠ ܕܒܪܐ ܛܒܐ ܘܡܘܡܝܢܐ ܟܠ ܡܟܝܠ ܡܘܡܝܢ
ܗܘܝܬ. ܟܠ ܥܣܩܘܬܐ ܐܡܝܢܐ ܗ̄ܝ ܟܠ ܢܦܫܬܐ ܡܬܒܥܝܬܐ ܕܒܝܫܬܐ ܐܠܗܝܬ
ܗܘܝܬ* ܡܘܡܝܢܐ. ܟܠ ܢܦܫܬܐ ܦܬܓܡܬܐ ܕܡܠܐܟܐ ܐܡܝܢ. ܒܟܠ ܟܝܢܘܗ̇
ܘܡܪܐ ܕܟܠ. ܐܝܟ ܕܐܡܪܢ ܕܠܐ ܙܡ ܘܠܐ ܡܫܟܚ ܠܐܣܘܬܐ ܕܢ̈ܦܫܐ ܘܕܡܫܬܪܝܬܐ
ܕܡܫܚܢ ܗܘ ܒܪܐ ܗܠܐ ܡܕܒܪܢܘܬܐ ܕܐܡܪܐ ܢܒܝܐ ܗܘ ܘܐܝܟܢܐ ܘܒܟܠܐ ܘܦܠܚܝܢ
ܕܐܝܟ ܒܗ ܕܢܒܝܝܢ ܕܢܦܪܝܢ ܩܕܡ ܒܒܪܐ. ܘܐܡܬܝ ܘܐܡܝܢܐ ܗܘܐ ܒܟܠܗܘܢ
ܒܡܫܘܬܐ ܗܘܐ ܕܠܐ ܡܬܡܨܝܐ. ܘܒܡܐ ܐܝܟܢܐ ܩܕܡ ܒܒܪܐ.
ܚܕܐ ܩܕܡܬܐ ܐܝܟܢܐ ܒܒ̈ܪܐ ܠܠܒܐ. ܩܕܡ ܘܒܒܪܐ ܐܝܟܢܐ ܗܠܐ ܠܠܒܐ ܗܘܐ
ܒܒ̈ܪܐ ܪܚܡܬܐ ܗܠܐ ܠܠܒ ܠܠܒ̈ܐ ܘܒܝܘܡܐ ܠܠܒ ܠܠܒܝܢ. ܘܣܘܒܠܬܐ ܕܗܘܐ
ܟܠ ܒܪܢܫܐ ܐܝܟ ܒܟܠܗܘܢ ܒܒ̈ܪܐ ܪ̈ܓܫܐ ܒܗܠܐ ܘܡܫܡܫ ܡܫܬܪܝܐ ܦܠܚܘܬܐ.
ܒܒ̈ܪܐ ܩܕܡܐ ܠܠܒܐ ܘܡܫܡܫܬܐ. ܦܠܚܢܐ ܩܕܡܐ ܠܠܒܐ ܘܡܫܡܫ ܗܠܐ ܗܘܐ
ܦܠ ܚܝܠܐ ܩܕܡܐ ܘܡܫܡܫ ܠܠܒܐ ܘܡܒܡܫܬܐ ܘܡܫܡܫ. ܒܒ̈ܪܐ ܡܢܝܐ ܗܘܐ
ܡܫܡܫܬܐ ܘܩܕܡܝܢ ܘܡܒܠܐ ܠܠܒܐ. ܘܡܫܡܫ ܪ̈ܓܫܐ ܘܩܕܡܫܬܐ ܠܠܒܐ ܘܡܫܡܫ
ܘܡܒܡܝܢ ܠܠܒܝܢ ܘܐܝܟ ܡܢܝܢܘܗܝ.
22. ܠܘܬ ܕܡܫܬܪܝܐ ܦܠ ܢܘܡܐ ܡܕܡܘܪܐ ܕܕܘܒ ܩܡ ܡܫܠܡܢܝܢ ܘܡܫܡܫܝܢ*
ܡܫܬܟܠܬܐ ܘܡܫܬܪܪܝܢܘܬܐ ܘܫܡ̈ܝܢܬܐ ܘܡܫܩܐ ܘܒܘܪ̈ܙܐ ܐܟܠܘܗܝ ܘܐܡܪ: ܡܒܝܢܝܢ
ܡܠܟܝܢܝܢ ܗܠܝܢ ܡܪ̈ܝܐ ܗܟܝܠ ܘܐܡܪܐ ܘܡܛܠ ܗܠܝܢ ܢܦܫ ܦܘܪܫܐ
ܕܢܒܝܝܢ ܗܘ ܘܐܝܟܢܐ ܘܒܢܘܗܝ ܘܦܠܚܝܢ ܕܐܝܟ ܒܗ ܕܢܦܪܘܢ.

Nobody will say it is good for a man to be sold in order to repay 10,000 (= myriad *-rebu* pl.) talents. Is a human being so great, and heaven and earth lesser than him? It is because he was created in the image of God. God the Father created him and gave him freedom, and authority over himself, honouring him more than anything He created and promising that he would seat him on the 'tenth (*'siroyo*) and exalted throne' above all angels and heavenly hosts.

Since he had disregarded the commandment of his Lord, he did not observe the regulations and the laws his Creator has set down for him, (that is) neither fasting, prayers nor prostrations which has been determined for him, the king ordered that he be sold along with his wife, children and everything he had.

Who is the buyer and what is sold? His transgressions and negligence are the price. The buyer is Satan, for he has sold himself for a great price to Satan [**49**], by separating himself from the dignity of the children and choosing servitude to Satan. Since he became a slave, he is no more free and no more has autonomy. As he has sold himself voluntarily by his transgression, and his wife – the gift of the Holy Spirit – is taken away from him and he has the spirit of servitude, instead of the Holy Spirit. The members of the Christian flock are his children, who call him their father. Since he had chosen servitude, fatherhood no more remains with him, and they have become children to another diligent father. And all that he has is the negligent services and prayers. He had offered the holy mysteries in ignorance and impiety, instead heedlessly and negligently. They are not reckoned to him, because he has performed them with negligence. By transgressions and violations of the regulations and the number (that is, of prayers and prostrations), he became a slave to Satan. No chance of repentance has been left for him, and hope for conversion has been cut off. He has become an heir to 'the outer darkness' (cfr. Matt. 22:13), along with demons as companions forever.

ܠܐ ܐܝܟ ܢܐܡܪ: ܟܡܐ ܛܒ ܒܪܢܫܐ ܕܝܕܥ ܕܢܦܪܘܫ ܪ̈ܚܡܘ ܚܒܪ̈ܐ. ܒܪܢܫܐ ܡܕܝܢ ܪܒܐ
ܐܠܗܘܗܝ ܘܡܟܡܐ ܘܐܪܒܐ ܒܪܝܫ ܡܕܝܢ. ܡܛܠ ܕܒܪܟܡܘ ܕܐܠܗܐ ܐܬܒܪܝ. ܒܪܝܘܗܝ
ܠܐܠܗܐ ܐܒܐ. ܘܡܘܒ ܠܗ ܚܐܘܪܬܐ ܘܡܠܟܘܬܐ ܟܡܠܬܐ ܘܡܦܪܗ ܛܒ ܡܢ ܦܠܚܝܢ
ܕܟܪܐ. ܘܐܬܡܠܘܗܝ ܠܗ ܕܠܟܠ ܡܢ ܦܠܚܘܗܝ ܡܠܐܟܐ ܘܦܠܚܘܬܐ ܡܫܝܚܝܬܐ
ܢܬܒܝܘܗܝ ܒܡܘܬܒܐ ܒܫܪܢܐ ܘܟܠܐ.
ܘܡܛܠ ܕܐܗܡܢ ܒܡܘܬܒܝ ܡܪܗ. ܘܠܐ ܫܡܠܝ ܐܣܝܡܐ ܘܡܬܩܢܐ ܕܫܩܠ ܠܗ
ܒܪܘܚܐ ܕܝܠܗ. ܘܠܐ ܙܘܥܐ ܘܠܐ ܪܚܡܬܐ ܘܡܚܫܒܬܐ ܕܐܬܬܚܝܒ ܠܗ. ܦܩܕ ܡܠܟܐ
ܕܝܕܥ ܗܘ ܕܐܝܬܘܬܐ ܘܒܢܝܐ ܘܦܠܚܝܢ ܕܐܝܬ ܠܗ.
ܦܡ ܐܠܗܘܗܝ ܐܘܒܠܐ ܘܒܡܘܡܝ ܡܕܝܢ: ܡܠܟܘܬܗ ܘܡܣܒܪܢܘܬܐ ܕܠܗ
ܘܠܝܢ ܐܢܫ ܠܡܫܡܫܘܬܗ. ܘܪܒܘܬܐ ܫܠܝܐ ܐܠܗܘܗܝ. ܡܛܠ ܕܗܘ ܐܝܟ ܢܡܘܣ
ܫܟܝܚܬܐ ܠܟܠܗ ܠܗܠܝܐ* ܒܐܘܪܚ ܢܠܗ ܡܢ ܕܘܟܐ ܕܩܒܠ ܡܠܠܐ ܠܗ
ܒܥܒܘܕܘܬܐ ܕܫܠܝܐ. ܘܡܛܠ ܕܗܘܐ ܟܒܝܪ ܠܐ ܦܩܕ ܠܗ ܚܐܘܪܬܐ ܘܠܐ ܡܫܒܚܬܐ
ܟܡܠܬܐ. ܡܛܠ ܕܗܘ ܒܪܟܢܗ ܐܝܟ ܢܡܘܣ ܒܡܠܟܘܬܗ ܘܐܝܬܘܬܗ ܡܫܘܚܬܐ
ܕܪܘܚܐ ܩܕܝܫܐ ܐܠܗܢܐ ܡܫܠܡܢܐ ܡܢܗ ܘܦܘܫܐ ܠܗ ܪܘܚܐ ܕܥܒܕܘܬܐ ܚܠܦ ܪܘܚܐ
ܩܕܝܫܐ ܐܠܗܢܐ. ܘܒܢܘܗܝ ܒܢ̈ܝ ܡܠܟܘܬܐ ܡܫܝܚܝܬܐ ܐܠܗܝܬܐ. ܘܗܢܘܢ ܕܡܢܢ
ܠܗ ܐܒܘܗܝ: ܡܛܠ ܕܩܒܠ ܠܗ ܥܒܕܘܬܐ ܠܐ ܦܩܕ ܠܗ ܐܒܘܬܐ. ܘܒܢܝܐ ܗܘܘ
ܠܝܪܬܘܬܐ ܐܒܐ ܫܡܝܐ. ܘܦܠܚܝܢ ܕܐܝܬ ܠܗ ܠܡܫܡܫܬܐ ܘܪ̈ܚܡܬܐ ܩܕܝܫܬܐ
ܐܠܗܘܗܝ. ܘܙܕܩ ܕܢܦܠ ܘܫܢܝܐ ܥܠ ܕܚܠܬܐ ܘܥܠ ܕܡܠܬܐ. ܐܠܐ ܐܝܟ ܕܐܬܐ
ܘܡ̈ܫܡܫܐ. ܘܠܝܢ ܠܐ ܡܬܚܫܒܝܢ ܠܗ ܡܛܠ ܕܒܦܘܪܫܢܐ ܗܟܢ ܐܢܘܢ.
ܘܡܠܟܘܬܐ ܒܒ̈ܢܝ. ܠܡܫܘܚܐ ܘܠܡܫܝܚܐ ܗܘܐ ܚܒܪܐ ܠܫܠܝܐ. ܘܠܐ ܦܩܕ
ܠܗ ܠܡܥܒܕ. ܘܐܬܦܩܕ ܡܫܪܐ ܕܡܠ̈ܟܘܬܐ. ܗܘܐ ܓܝܪ ܕܩܢܘܡܐ ܟܝܢܐ ܒܢ
ܫܪܝܐ ܒ̈ܢܝܗ ܠܟܠܗܘܢ ܒܢܝܢ܀

23. *Another interpretation*:

Rebutho (a Myriad) is ten thousand. The talent is the *Qurbono*, or the holy Body and the absolving Blood **[50]** which is offered everyday forever in the Holy Church of the earth-born. A priest ought to minister (*nkahen*) and serve (*nshamesh*) and offer (*nqareb*) the divine mysteries for thirty years, and if he has strength in bodily composition, he shall continue as long as he can, and because the days of a year are 365, ten years will be 3,650 days. Thirty years make 10,950 days. If the days of fasting are reduced from it, every year 32 days and in 10 years 320 days, and in 30 years 960 days, there remains 9,990 (days). And every four years one day shall be added from the course of the sun, which is called a leap year. In thirty years seven and a half days, making the days in which he ought to offer in thirty years 9,997. And the consecration of the divine Myron is celebrated making 10,000. In all the days of his priesthood, a priest shall be present on the occasion of the offering of the holy Mysteries. If he offers or he is present, he completes 10,000 times being present for the holy Mysteries **[51]**. If he is negligent (to be present), he owes 10,000 talents on the day when he has nothing to repay.

It is not right that a priest is present at the time of the mysteries without completing the prayers and prostrations that are prescribed: *Ramsho*, *Sutoro*, four services of *Lilyo*, *Sapro* and third hour, and then he shall be present at the time of the divine Mysteries. After the Mysteries, in the ninth hour, he shall commemorate the departed. If he is present for the *Qurbono* without completing prayers and prostrations, he will be a lazy and avaricious person who seeks the granary without laboring or sowing, or cleansing the seedlings (from tares), and without reaping and has not (even) brought the ears of the wheat to the granary, and wants to take the wheat home.

23. ܦܘܫܩܐ ܐ̱ܚܪܢܐ: ܪ̈ܘܚܐܠܒܢ̈ܝܐ ܠܟܠܢܫܐ ܐܝܬܘܬܗ. ܘܒܪܐ ܐܝܬܘܬܗ ܡܘܕܥܐ
ܐܘܟܝܬ ܦܓܪܐ ܩܕܝܫܐ ܘܕܡܐ* ܡܚܝܢܐ. ܕܟܠ ܝܘܡܐ ܐܡܝܢܐܝܬ ܡܬܩܪܒ
ܒܥܕܬܐ ܩܕܝܫܬܐ ܕܐܘܪܚܝܐ. ܒܟܠ ܕܪܘܫ ܠܥܘܢܐ ܠܥܠܡܝܢ ܚܝ̈ܐ ܢܬܠ ܘܢܫܒܘܩ
ܘܢܥܕܪ ܠܐܘܪܐ ܠܟܠܢܫܐ. ܘܐܦ ܐܝܟ ܒܗ ܚܝܠܐ ܕܪܘܚܐ ܦܓܪܢܝܐ ܢܘܣܦ ܟܡܐ
ܕܡܪܐ ܘܡܫܠܛ ܕܢܘܗܪܐ ܕܚܝܠܐ ܐܝܟ ܡܐ ܘܗܟܢ ܘܢܣܒܘܢ ܐܝܬܘܗܝ. ܒܗܢܐ
ܡܢܐ ܐܝܟܢܐ ܠܟܠܢܫܐ ܘܗܟܢ ܡܐ ܘܢܣܒܘܢ ܢܘܗܪܐ ܢܗܘܘܢ. ܒܠܠܟܝܢ ܡܢܐ
ܒܗܢܐ ܠܟܠܡܢܐ ܘܐܝܟ ܡܐ ܘܢܣܒܘܢ ܢܘܗܪܐ ܠܒܝܫܘܢ. ܢܗܘܐ ܡܢܗܘܢ ܢܘܗܪܐ
ܕܪܘܚܐ ܕܟܠ ܚܝܠܐ ܐܝܟܢܐ ܘܐܙܝܢ ܢܘܚܐ. ܒܒܗܢܐ ܡܢܐ ܐܝܟܢܐ ܡܐ ܘܒܗܢܝܢ
ܢܘܗܪܐ. ܒܠܠܟܝܢ ܡܢܐ ܐܝܬܘܬܐ ܘܗܟܢ ܢܘܗܪܐ. ܦܐܝܢ ܐܝܬܝܐ ܠܟܠܢܫܐ
ܘܐܝܬܘܬܐ ܘܐܝܬܝܢ. ܘܒܟܠ ܐܘܪܚܐ ܡܢܐ ܠܐܠܗܐ ܢܘܗܪܐ ܚܕܐ ܡܢ ܗܘܒܐ
ܕܡܫܐ. ܘܢܥܕܪܘܢ ܚܝܠܐ ܒܚܝܠܬܐ. ܒܠܠܟܝܢ ܡܢܐ ܡܒܪܐ ܢܘܗܪܐ ܘܦܓܪܐ.
ܗܘܝܢ ܢܘܗܪܐ ܕܒܗܘܢ ܪܘܚ ܕܡܬܩܪܒ ܒܠܠܟܝܢ ܡܢܐ ܐܝܬܝܐ ܠܟܠܢܫܐ
ܘܐܝܬܘܬܐ ܘܐܝܬܝܢ ܘܡܒܪܐ. ܘܗܘܝܘ ܡܘܙܓ ܠܟܘܠܐ ܡܫܡܠܠ ܒܒܗܢܐ ܠܟܠܢܫܐ.
ܪܘܚ ܒܒܗܘܢ ܕܦܓܪܗܘܢ ܢܘܗܪ ܒܗܘܬܐ ܠܡܠܟܐ ܒܒܪܐ ܕܡܬܩܪܒܝܢ ܪ̈ܙܐ
ܩܕ̈ܝܫܐ. ܐܦ ܗܘ ܢܥܕܪ ܘܐܠܐ ܠܡܠܟܐ ܕܢܫܡܠܐ ܕܒܗܢܐ ܠܟܠܢܫܐ ܕܒܢ̈ܝܐ ܐܬܠܟܐ
ܒܒܪܐ ܕܪ̈ܙܐ ܩܕ̈ܝܫܐ.* ܐܢܫܝܢ ܢܗܘܐ ܠܡܐܟܠ ܡܢܗ ܪ̈ܟܢ ܒܒܪܐ ܒܗܘܬܐ ܒܡܠܟܘܬܗ
ܡܢܗ ܠܥܦܪܐ.
ܘܐܦ ܠܐ ܪܘܚ ܒܒܗܘܢ ܕܡܠܟܐ ܒܒܢ ܪ̈ܙܐ ܒܢܘܗܪ ܕܢܫܡܠܐ ܙܒ̈ܢܐ ܘܦܬܓ̈ܡܐ
ܕܒܗܘܢ ܡܬܝܚܝܢ. ܘܪܘܚܐ ܘܗܘܝܘܐ ܘܐܘܪܚܐ ܠܐܝܬܘܬܐ ܕܟܠܗ ܘܦܓܪܐ ܘܐܝܬܗ
ܡܬܝܢ. ܘܗܘܝܢ ܠܡܠܟܐ ܒܒܢ ܪ̈ܙܐ ܠܟܘܬܐ. ܘܒܠܒ ܪ̈ܙܐ ܒܠܟܘܬ ܡܢܝܢ ܠܟܘܢ
ܒܢܝܬܐ. ܐܢܝܢ ܠܡܠܟܐ ܒܡܘܪܒܐ ܒܝ ܠܐ ܡܥܒܕ ܙܒ̈ܢܐ ܘܦܬܓ̈ܡܐ ܡܠܝܐ
ܒܢܚܝܐ ܡ̈ܚܝܐ ܕܚܠܐ ܐܘ̈ܪܐ. ܒܝ ܠܐ ܦܠܓܝ ܘܠܐ ܪܘܚܐ ܘܠܐ ܕܒ ܪܘܚܗ. ܘܠܐ ܡܪܘܓ. ܘܠܐ
ܐܝܟ ܡܟܠܠ ܠܐܘܪܐ ܘܪܒܐ ܕܫ̈ܡܝܐ ܢܚܡܐ ܒܚܝܠܗ.

One who completes all of them (= prayers) and is not present at the time of the Mysteries, resembles a foolish man who has laboured, sowed, cleansed the seedlings from tares and weeds, reaped and brought the ears of wheat to the granary and left it there for people to tread on and it is wasted, without his getting any profit from his labours. One who completes all prayers and prostrations and is present at the time of the holy Mysteries resembles a wise man who is not shaken by the storms of this disorderly world, and whose boat reached the harbor of peace.

24. *Exposition of the prayers and their numbers following the concept of the sower:*

First prayer of *Ramsho* is the tilling and the second prayer, of *Sutoro* is [**52**] the sowing. The third, fourth and fifth and sixth – the four *nocturns* (*edonne*) of *Lilyo* are the cleansing of the seedlings, from tares and weeds, thorns and thistles. The seventh prayer of *Sapro* is harvesting, the eighth prayer of the third hour is bringing in of the wheat, the ninth prayer of the sixth hour is ingathering of the wheat into the storehouse. The tenth prayer of the ninth hour is almsgiving from first-fruits of the (winnowed) wheat for the living and the dead, or for the righteous and the sinners.

ܘܐܝܟܐ ܕܡܫܡܫܠܐ ܗܘܬ ܩܕܡܝܗܘܢ: ܟܕܝ ܙ̈ܐܪܐ ܠܐ ܡܬܦܫܩܢ ܡܬܦܪܫܐ ܠܟܬܒܐ
ܗܝܟܠܐ: ܕܦܬܚ ܘܐܪܕܝ ܘܢܦܩ ܪܘܚܗ ܡܢ ܦܓܪܐ ܘܡܫܟܢܐ. ܘܫܪܝ ܐ̈ܬܘܬܐ ܘܐܬܘܬܐ
ܡܟܠ ܠܒܪܐ ܘܡܚܡܟܗ ܩܕܡ ܕܩ̈ܢܐ ܘܐܟܢ. ܘܡܚܕ ܠܐ ܐܬܚܙܝ ܡܢ ܟܠܗ. ܘܐܝܟܐ
ܕܡܫܡܫܠܐ ܩܕܡܝܗܘܢ ܕܥ̈ܠܬܐ ܘܡܫܬܡܠܝܢ ܟܕܝ ܙ̈ܐܪܐ ܩܕ̈ܝܫܐ ܡܬܦܪܫܐ
ܠܒܢܝܐ ܠܟܠܡܐ ܕܠܐ ܐܪ̈ܐܝ ܡܢ ܒܐܬܘܬܗܘܢ ܕܟܠܗܘܢ ܗܘܐ ܥܠܝܡܐ ܘܐܟܠܗ
ܐܬܚܒܫ ܠܟܠܗܝ ܟܢܫܐ.

24. ܡܘܕܥܢܘܬܐ ܕܥ̈ܠܬܐ ܘܡܫܠܡܝܢ ܐܝܟ ܥܢܝܢܐ ܕܙܘ̈ܙܐ:
ܥܠܬܐ ܩܕܡܝܬܐ ܕܪܫܡܐ ܐܠܗܐ ܕܦܘܠܚܢܐ. ܘܥܠܬܐ ܠܪܘܚܢܝܬܐ ܕܫܘܬܦܐ
ܐܠܗܐ* ܕܪܘܚܐ. ܘܐܬܒܠܥܬܐ ܘܪܒܝܥܝܬܐ ܘܡܣܬܒܥܝܬܐ ܘܡܬܬܠܬܐ ܐܪܒܥܐ ܟܪ̈ܝܐ
ܕܟܠܗ ܐܠܗܘܢ ܕܗܘܐ ܕܪܘܚܐ ܡܢ ܐܪ̈ܙܐ ܘܡܕܒܪܐ ܘܡܢ ܟܦ̈ܢܐ ܘܙܪ̈ܥܐ. ܘܥܠܬܐ
ܡܫܝܚܝܬܐ ܕܦܓܪܐ ܐܠܗܐ ܕܝܠܗ. ܘܥܠܬܐ ܠܡܫܝܚܝܬܐ ܕܐܬܠܗ ܡܢ ܐܠܗܐ
ܕܡܫܠܐ. ܘܥܠܬܐ ܠܡܫܝܚܝܬܐ ܕܡܫܚ ܡܢ ܐܠܗܐ ܐܒܐ ܘܡ̈ܬܚܫܒܢܐ ܠܡܦܩܢܐ.
ܘܥܠܬܐ ܟܢܫܬܢܝܬܐ ܕܐܬܩܪܝ ܡܢ ܐܠܗܐ ܕܝܠܗ ܕܗܘܐ ܡܢ ܥܡܝܬܐ ܕܐܪܙܐ
ܐܠܗ ܐܢܫܐ ܘܡܬܦܠܓܐ ܐܟܚܕܐ ܕܪ̈ܫܐ ܘܡܫܬܐ.

25. *A clarification regarding the commencement of the prayers*:

Many of the doctors of the Church say that *Sapro* is the commencement of the prayers as far as they have understood without having investigated the details of the matter. Rather, having observed that people wash their hands and face and go to the (service of) prayer, they supposed that *Sapro* is the beginning of the day and (also) at the beginning of the prayers, not realizing that washing is a different matter: people wash their faces and hands and feet[40] every morning, and they do not know what they are doing; but as they have seen what their forefathers doing, they imitate them. And they do not know that they are washing the five external senses, and with them they also remember the internal ones lest **[53]** they be guilty during that day.

Why do people wash in the morning and not in the evening? Because in the night, secretions of the body are gathered up in him, in five external senses through which the worldly things enter a person. (Therefore) a person ought to cleanse their senses when they wake up from the night's sleep: they should wash them with water and with supplications. (As) they wash their hands, eyes, ears, nostrils and mouth, they should say, "I have washed my hands before You O God, so that they be stretched forth for doing good, and not for the practice of what is hateful; and so that my eyes may see what is upright, and not become corrupted, and that my ears may hear your commandments, and not heed to obscene things, and that my nostrils may inhale the fragrance of Your salvation, and not the odours of laxity and my mouth may experience thanksgiving and praises and not speak haughtily or (utter) falsehood".

---

[40] The manuscript has 'and their feet' in brackets.

25. ܟܪܘܙܘ ܟܪܘܙܝ ܙܟܘ̈ܬܐ: ܫܦܝܪܬܐ ܡܢ ܡܠܟܘܬܐ ܕܒܝܬܐ ܐܡܪܗ ܕܙܟܘܬܐ
ܐܠܗܗ ܚܘܪܐ ܕܙܟܘܬܐ ܐܝܟܢܐ ܕܐܘܪܚܗ. ܟܕ ܠܐ ܚܙܝܗ ܟܠ ܚܠܝܠܘܬܐ ܫܦܝܪܐ
ܕܡܠܟܗܘܢ. ܐܠܐ ܟܕ ܚܙܘ ܠܟܢܫܐ ܕܒܗ ܙܒܢܐ ܡܫܡܫܝܢ ܐܝܩܪܘܗܝ ܘܐܦܩܘܗܝ ܘܐܙܠܘ
ܠܒܝܬܐ ܡܪܗ ܕܙܒܢܐ ܐܠܗܘܗܝ ܚܘܒܐ ܕܡܘܬܐ ܘܚܘܒܐ ܕܙܟܘܬܐ ܘܠܐ ܐܘܪܚܗ
ܕܡܢܝܚܬܐ ܡܢ ܩܕܡ ܐܠܗܗ. ܘܫܦܝܪܬܐ ܡܫܡܫܝܢ ܐܦܣܩܘܢ ܘܐܬܪܝܡܘܢ
(ܘܩܒܠܘܗܝ) ܒܟܠ ܙܒܢ. ܘܠܐ ܐܬܕܟܪ ܡܢܐ ܚܛܝܢ. ܐܠܐ ܐܦܠܐ ܕܡܪܗ ܠܐܒܗܬܗܘܢ
ܘܥܒܕܘ ܒܟܠܗ ܐܝܩܪܗܘܢ. ܘܠܐ ܚܒܝܫ ܕܢܣܡܟܐ ܩܘܡܐ ܒܢܝܐ ܡܫܡܫܝܢ ܘܟܗܢܐ
ܒܗܘܢ ܡܢܗܘܢ ܘܠܐ* ܢܬܚܫܒܘܢ ܒܗ ܒܢܡܘܣܐ.
ܘܡܫܬܒܚܝܢ ܒܙܢܐ ܡܫܡܫܝܢ ܒܪܘܚܐ ܘܠܗ ܒܙܡܪܐ. ܟܠ ܕܒܠܠܐ ܡܬܠܒܫܝܢ
ܒܗ ܡܠܦܢܘܬܐ ܕܫܦܪܐ ܒܫܡܫܐ ܩܘܡܐ ܟܢܫܐ ܕܗܘܘ ܚܠܝܡ ܒܚܝܠܐ ܠܟܠܝܠܐ
ܟܠ ܒܢܝܐ. ܙܕܩ ܠܗ ܠܟܢܫܐ ܕܟܕ ܦܐܡ ܡܢ ܡܠܬܐ ܠܡܫܡܫܘܬܐ ܕܗܘܐ ܩܘܡܐ
ܕܠܗ. ܘܡܫܡܫܝܢ ܐܝܟ ܒܢܝܐ ܘܒܢܬܐ. ܡܫܡܫܝܢ ܐܝܩܪܘܗܝ ܘܡܫܒܚܝܢ ܘܐܘܕܝܘܗܝ
ܘܫܒܚܘܗܝ ܘܦܪܣܘ ܘܐܡܪܘ ܐܝܟ ܡܠܬܐ ܐܬܝܐ ܡܫܡܫܝܢ ܠܐܠܗܐ ܕܢܬܦܣܩܘܢ
ܠܡܫܘܕܥܘ ܢܦܫܬܐ ܘܒܗ ܠܡܫܘܠܡܐ ܘܡܢܬܬܐ ܘܒܢܝܢ ܕܫܪܝܢ ܐܘܪܚܬܐ ܘܠܐ ܢܦܫܝ
ܕܒܢܝܢܬܐ. ܘܐܘܪܝܢ ܕܒܪܝܬܐ ܠܡܫܒܝܢܘܗܝ ܘܠܐ ܢܦܩܘܢ ܡܢ ܬܪܥܐ. ܘܢܣܒܘܗܝ
ܕܢܡܘܣܐ ܙܢܝܐ ܕܦܘܪܫܢ. ܘܠܐ ܒܝܫܬܐ ܕܙܢܘܬܐ. ܘܦܘܠܚܢ ܕܢܝܚܢ ܠܐܘܪܚܬܐ
ܘܠܡܟܝܢܬܐ ܘܠܐ ܢܥܠܢܘܢܗ ܕܒܝܫܬܐ.

And with the purification of the outer senses, a person cleanses the inner senses which are the mind, understanding, conscience, intelligence and intellect. Then he shall go to the church and pray and shall go out for worldly activities, fulfilling the promises of the morning, when he promised not to become guilty in anything before God.

Why does man not wash in the evening? **[54]** Because the secretions have not accumulated in them during the day, but they cleanse them little by little. Another (reason): because they are not going off to some worldly business, but to sleeping and rest. And when he rises up in the night[41] for prayer, if they wash, it is good; if they do not wash, they are not blameworthy, because they are not going off for (some) worldly business, cleansing their senses from detestable works. Rather they are going for prayer and praises (hymns) which are purifiers of the soul and the body, because by the cleansing of the body alone, soul is not purified: even if (the body) is washed in the water of the ocean, the soul is not purified, for the washing of the body is for the cleansing of the bodily dirt while the washing of the soul cleanses from the blemishes of the soul and the body. A person does not need washing of their limbs every day apart from the five external senses, which are the entrance for the evil passions in a person. With their washing (of the limbs), a person recalls the five internal senses that they may be set free from the evils of the day, while the rest of the limbs are washed from external dirt.

[41] Or 'at *Lilyo*'.

ܘܥܡ ܕܫܘܩܐ ܕܦ̈ܓܪܐ ܒܬ̈ܐ ܡܕܝܢܐ ܠܬ̈ܓܪܐ ܩܫ̈ܝܐ. ܕܐܝܬܝܗܘܢ ܗܘܝܢ ܘܡܕܝܢܬܐ ܘܙܟܝܐ. ܠܐܪܚܡܬܐ. ܡܕܝܢܐ. ܘܒܬܪܟܢ ܢܐܙܠ ܠܒܝܬܐ ܘܕܠܐ ܢܫܘܡ ܠܫܘܒ̈ܚܢܐ ܠܠܩ̈ܢܝܐ. ܡܢ ܡܫܡܫܢܐ ܡܗܘܝܢܐ ܙܒ̈ܢܐ ܕܐܬܠܘܢ ܕܠܐ ܢܬܚܝܒ ܒܥܒܕ ܡܕܡ ܠܚܘܐ.

ܘܡܬܚܫܒܐ ܒܪܫܡܐ ܠܐ ܡܫܡܥܝܢ ܒܪܢܫܐ. ܒܟܠ* ܕܠܐ ܡܬܕܒܪܝܢ ܒܗ ܬܠܡ̈ܝܕܘܬܐ ܒܐܡܢܐ. ܐܠܐ ܒܡܡܠܠ ܡܡܠܠ ܡܕܝܢܐ ܠܗܘܢ. ܘܐܣܪܐ ܕܠܐ ܠܫܘܒ̈ܚܢܐ ܠܠܥܡܐ ܐܝܟ: ܐܠܐ ܠܥܡܠܐ ܘܥܡܠܐ. ܘܐܡܠܟܘ ܕܢܐܡ ܒܟܠܗ ܠܪܓܘܬܐ. ܐܢ ܢܥܝܢ ܠܗ ܢܗܘܐ. ܘܐܢ ܠܐ ܢܥܝܢ ܠܐ ܢܬܩܒܠ ܕܒܗ ܠܫܘܒ̈ܚܢܐ[42] ܠܠܩ̈ܢܝܐ ܐܝܟ ܕܒܥܐ ܩ̈ܢܘܗܝ ܡܢ ܦܘܠܚܢܐ ܕܚ̈ܛܝܬܐ. ܐܠܐ ܐܝܟ ܠܪܓܘܬܐ ܘܠܡܬܚܫܒܬܐ ܕܐܝܬܝܗܝܢ ܡܕܒܪ̈ܢܝܬܐ ܕܢܦܫܐ ܘܦܓܪܐ ܕܒܗܘܢܐ ܕܦܓܪܐ ܟ̇ܠܗܘܢ ܠܐ ܡܬܕܒܪܐ ܢܦܫܐ. ܘܐܢ ܡܬܬܐܡܝܢ ܒܥܒ̈ܕܐ ܕܢܦܫܐ ܠܐ ܡܬܕܒܪܐ ܢܦܫܐ. ܘܡܪܓܫܢܘܬܐ ܕܦܓܪܐ ܠܡܘܫܚܬܐ ܦܓܪܢܝܬܐ ܡܕܒܪܐ. ܘܡܪܓܫܢܘܬܐ ܕܢܦܫܐ ܠܡܫ̈ܘܚܬܐ ܘܦܓܪܐ ܡܕܒܪܢܐ. ܒܪܢܫܐ ܠܐ ܡܫܟܚ ܒܟܠ ܡܪܓܫܬܐ ܕܩ̈ܘܡܐ ܥܠ ܚܕܐ ܕܗܠܝܢ ܡܢ ܦ̈ܓܪܐ ܢ̈ܦܫܐ ܟ̈ܬܒܐ ܘܐܝܬܝܗܘܢ ܡܕܒܪ̈ܢܐ ܕܢܦܫܐ ܒܦ̈ܓܪܐ ܟܠ ܒܪܢܫܐ. ܘܡܢ ܦܓܪܝܗܘܢ ܡܕܒܪܘ ܠܡܫܡܫܐ ܦ̈ܓܪܐ ܟ̈ܬܒܐ ܕܢܬܚܙܘܢ ܡܢ ܒܥܡܠܗ ܕܢܦܫܐ. ܘܡܢܐ ܕܦ̈ܓܪܐ ܡܢ ܐ̈ܬܐ ܒ̈ܢܝܬܐ ܡܬܐܡܝܢ.

---

[42] Ms ܫܘܒ̈ܚܢܐ.

There is no movement (involved) for them,[43] except by the five senses, as we have mentioned. When a nocturnal pollution occurs for someone, or in intercourse, let them wash and if possible take a bath and fast on **[55]** that day, not because he was defiled, but for the honour of the prayer, for it is not right that someone draws near to prayer while unclean: on that day, he shall not offer (Eucharist) nor draw near (to receive communion?). If something else happens, the washing does not cleanse, nor bath, because washing and bathing do not cleanse from sin, but only from the bodily defilement. Without tears and repentance, sin is not cleansed.

26. [*Various matters*]:

Again the secular priests ought to observe[44] Wednesday, Friday and Sunday, feasts of the Lord, commemoration of the saints and the martyrs. Anyone who violates is cursed before God.

Again, a priest who approaches his wife when she is pregnant is a pagan and his *Qurbono* is not accepted. Again, when a human being comes to be formed (in the womb) they dwell, nine months in darkness, and then they come out to see the light of the earth like their mother.

The beginning of the prayer of all the days of a year is the first prayer of *Ramsho*; (this) is known from the prayers and services of the Church that the fathers and doctors of old have set down and ordered in the Holy Church. The stewards of the Church begin the feasts of the Lord with *Ramsho* **[56]** with the prayers and services of the feasts; and again on Sundays, their prayers and services begin with *Ramsho*; and all the days of the year, they commence prayer and their service for the day with *Ramsho*. And Moses, the head of the prophets, said: "There was evening and there was morning, the first day" (Gen 1:5), making evening precede morning.

---

[43] That is, the internal senses.

[44] Lit. 'keep themselves', from intercourse with their wives.

ܟܠܗ ܒܗܘܢ ܫܬܠܡܢܘܬܐ ܐܠܐ ܒܣܘܟܠܐ ܩܕܝܫܐ ܕܚܘܪܝܢ. ܘܐܬܠܠ ܕܢܬܒܪܟ
ܠܒܪܢܫܐ ܩܢܝܐ ܕܟܠܗܐ ܐܘ ܗܘܐ ܒܘܘܟܠ ܢܬܠܡܝܢ. ܘܐܦ ܡܕܡ ܢܗܝܪܐ ܘܚܙܐ*
ܗ̈ܘ[45] ܡܘܡܐ. ܠܗ ܟܠ ܕܐܫܬܡܥ ܐܠܐ ܠܐܡܪܐ ܕܪܥܘܬܐ. ܕܠܐ ܙܘܥ ܕܢܬܡܪܒ ܐܝܟ
ܟܪܣܬܐ ܡܢ ܠܐ ܕܝܠ. ܘܟܘܢ ܣܘܡܐ ܠܐ ܢܙܘܥ ܘܠܐ ܢܬܪܒ. ܘܐܦ ܡܕܡ ܐܝܬ
ܢܗܘܐ. ܡܢܛܠ ܠܐ ܡܕܡܐ ܠܗ ܐܟܠܐ ܡܫܬܐ. ܟܠ ܕܡܢܛܠ ܘܡܫܬܐ ܠܐ
ܡܕܡܝ ܡܢ ܣܓܝܐܬܐ. ܐܠܐ ܡܢ ܡܘܣܝܬܐ ܦܪܝܫܬܐ ܠܣܘܪ. ܘܟܘܠܗ̇ ܡܢ ܕܩܕܡ
ܘܐܬܟܘܠ ܣܓܝܐܬܐ ܠܐ ܡܬܝܕܥܐ.

26. ܘܐܬܐ ܕܝܢ ܠܟܘܠܗ ܕܟܠܡܐ ܕܢܬܪܝܢ ܢܦܩܘܗܝ ܕܠܘܟܠ ܒܣܟܐ
ܘܟܪܘܟܬܐ ܘܟܝܢ ܒܣܟܐ ܘܟܬܒܐ ܡܥܝܢܐ ܘܕܘܟܪܢܐ ܕܡܕܥܐ ܘܕܝܢܐ. ܗ̈ܕܝܐ
ܕܗܟܢܐ ܗܘܐ ܠܡܢܐ ܡܕܡ ܠܟܠܗ.

ܘܐܬܐ ܒܗܢܐ ܕܡܬܡܪܒ ܠܐܝܬܘܗܝ ܡܢ ܗܘ ܟܠܗܝ ܒܥܘܕܐ ܐܬܬܗ ܘܡܘܪܒܢܗ ܠܐ
ܡܬܡܟܟ. ܘܐܬܐ ܒܪܢܫܐ ܐܡܬܐ ܕܐܬܐ ܠܒܘܡܟܐ ܠܐܡܟܐ ܚܝܝܐ ܟܡܪ ܒܣܘܡܟܐ
ܘܒܬܪܘܢ ܢܩܡ ܠܒܣܝܐ ܢܗܘܐ ܐܝܟ ܐܡܘ ܐܪܒܐ.

ܗܘܪܝ ܙܒܢܬܐ ܕܦܠܓܘܢ ܢܩܦܝ ܚܝܠܐ. ܙܒܢܬܐ ܡܕܡܝܬܐ ܕܪܡܫܐ ܐܬܠܝܗ ܘܡܕܟܐ
ܡܢ ܙܒܢ̈ܬܐ ܘܐܦܡܝܬܐ ܕܒܐܬܝܬܐ ܕܫܡܗ ܐܒܗ̈ܬܐ ܘܡܟܠܦܝܐ ܡܕܡܝܐ ܘܐܦܫܗ
ܒܕܒܬܐ ܡܕܝܡܬܐ. ܕܠܐܘܐ ܡܥܝܢܐ ܡܢ ܙܘܡܐ ܡܡܪܝܢ ܩܕܡ ܩܠܬܐ ܕܒܬܐ* ܒܙܒܢ̈ܬܐ
ܘܒܠܦܡܝܬܐ ܕܡܠܗܘܢ ܕܠܐܘܐ. ܘܡܣܒܪܡܐ. ܬܘܒ ܡܢ ܙܘܡܐ ܡܡܪܝܢ ܙܒܢ̈ܬܐ
ܘܬܦܩܝܬܐ ܕܡܠܗܘܢ. ܘܦܦܠܗܘܢ ܢܩܦܝ ܚܝܠܐ ܡܢ ܙܘܡܐ ܡܡܪܝܢ ܙܒܢܬܐ
ܘܬܦܡܝܬܐ ܕܡܠܗ ܕܢܘܡܐ. ܘܡܘܡܐ ܙܢܝܐ ܕܒܟܝܐ ܐܡܪ. ܘܗܘܐ ܙܘܡܐ ܗܘܐ ܙܒܢܐ
ܢܘܡܐ ܚܕ. ܡܕܡܘ ܠܪܘܡܐ ܟܠ ܙܒܢܐ.

[45] Ms ܘܗ ܘܗ̈.

Again, in the beginning, God created heaven and earth and earth was without form and void (Gen. 1:2), that is invisible and it was in the midst of with water, and darkness was upon the face of the deep[46] (Gen. 1:2), that is, prior to the earth. And when He said: Let dry land appear it rose above water (of) the deep and it saw the light appeared. And a human being, who comes to be formed dwells for nine months in darkness and then comes out to see the light, like the earth, his mother.

The prophet David said: "He made darkness and it was night, during which all the beasts of the forest go out: the lions roar to tear (their prey), seeking their food from God. At sun rise they go back and lie down in their dwellings. Man goes out for his work and to his labour until evening" (Ps. 104:20–23).

Again he said, "God save me in the evening, morning and noon" (Ps. 55:16–17; *Pesh*): the prophet begins with evening and ends with noon **[57]** in order to confirm that the prayer of *Ramsho* is the beginning of the prayers and that their ending is noon, that is, midday.

Qurbana is the completion (*shulomo*) of the holy Mysteries of the Church. As the Gospel is the 'seal' (*hutomo*) of the Old and New (Testaments). *Qurbana* is the 'seal' (*hutomo*) of all services. And the prayer of the Ninth hour is the confession and thanksgiving to God for all that God has abundantly given to all the children of the Holy Church.

The holy Gospel says, 'On Saturday evening, on Sunday dawn' (Matt. 28:1), that is, the ending of Saturday and the beginning of Sunday. (Here also) evening precedes morning and evening was the beginning of the day. It has been confirmed that prayers and services of the evening (*Ramsho*) are the beginning of the ten prayers that are completed in a day.

END

---

[46] The ms erroneously has *ṯhumo* 'limit, regulation', instead of *thumo*, 'depth'.

ܘܐܦ ܐܡܪ: ܒܪܫܝܬ ܒܪܐ ܐܠܗܐ ܝܬ ܫܡܝܐ ܘܝܬ ܐܪܥܐ. ܐܪܥܐ ܗܘܬ ܬܘܗ ܘܒܘܗ ܐܘܟܝܬ ܠܐ ܡܬܚܙܝܢܝܬܐ ܐܝܬܝܗ̇ ܗ̱ܘܬ ܟܣܝܐ ܡܝܐ. ܘܚܫܘܟܐ ܥܠ ܐܦܝ ܬܗܘܡܐ[47] ܗ̄ ܦܝܪܫ ܥܠ ܐܪܥܐ. ܟܕ ܕܝܢ ܐܡܪ ܠܐܬܪܐ ܡ̈ܪܚܦܢܝܬܐ ܡܪܚܦ ܥܠ ܐܦ̈ܝ ܡ̈ܝܐ ܠܬܗܘܡܐ ܘܚܫܟ ܢܘܗܪܐ. ܘܒܪܢܫܐ ܕ̇ܐܬܐ ܠܒܘܟܪܐ ܠܡܟܐ ܢ̈ܫܐ ܠܥܡܪ ܒܚܫܘܟܐ ܘܒܠܘܥܝ ܢܦܩ ܠܚܝܐ ܢܘܗܪܐ ܐܝܟ ܐܡܪܗ ܐܪܥܐ.

ܘܗܢܐ ܕܝܢ ܐܡܪ ܣܡܬ ܚܫܘܟܐ ܘܗܘܐ ܠܠܝܐ ܘܒܗ ܪ̈ܚܫܝܢ ܟܠܗܘܢ ܚ̈ܝܘܬܐ ܕܥܒܐ ܐܪ̈ܝܘܬܐ ܢܗܡܝܢ ܠܡܚܛܦ: ܘܠܡܒܥܐ ܡܢ ܐܠܗܐ ܡܐܟܘܠܬܗܘܢ. ܟܕ ܕܢܚ ܫ̄ܡܫܐ ܡܬܟܢܫܝܢ ܘܒܡܥܪ̈ܝܗܘܢ ܪܒܥܝܢ. ܢܦܩ ܒܪܢܫܐ ܠܥܒܕܗ ܘܠܦܘܠܚܢܗ ܥܕܡܐ ܠܪܡܫܐ.

ܘܐܦ ܐܡܪ: ܐܠܗܐ ܢܦܪܘܫ ܒܪܩܝܥܐ ܘܒܢܗܪ̈ܐ ܘܒܟܘܟ̈ܒܐ. ܘܡܢ ܪܩܝܥܐ ܗܢܐ ܢܗܘܐ ܘܟܘܟ̈ܒܐ ܗܟܢ* ܕܠܡܬܪܘܢ ܕܢ̈ܗܝܪܬܐ ܕܪܩܝܥܐ ܐܝܬܝܗ̇ ܫܡܫܐ ܕܢ̈ܗܝܪܬܐ ܘܟܘܟܒܐ ܕܐܝܬ̈ܝܗ ܦܠܓܗ ܕܝܘܡܐ ܡܫܠܛܢܘܢ.

ܥܠ ܕܡܫܪܒܠܐ ܡܫܠܛܐ ܐܝܬܝܗܘܢ ܕܬܪ̈ܬܐ ܦܢܝܬܐ ܕܥܠܡܐ. ܐܡܪܐ ܕܐܘܪ̈ܚܬܗܘܢ ܐܝܬܝܗܘܢ ܡܫܠܛܢܐ ܕܡܠܟܘܬܐ ܘܕܘܒܪܐ: ܗܟܢܐ ܡܕܒܪܢܐ ܐܝܬܝܗ̇ ܡܫܠܛܢܐ ܕܦܠܓܝܢ ܠܡܫܠܛܢܐ. ܘܟܘܟ̈ܒܐ ܕܠܡܫܡܫܢ ܡܕܒܪܢܘܬܐ ܘܡܫܬܥܒܕܢܘܬܐ ܠܐܠܗܐ ܐܝܬܝܗ̇. ܥܠ ܡܐ ܕܐܡܫܐ ܠܦܠܓܗܘܢ ܒܢ̈ܝܗ ܕܝܘܡܐ ܡܫܘܚܬܐ.

ܘܐܘܟܝܬ ܡܕܡܐ ܐܡܪ ܒܪܩܝܥܐ ܕܝܢ ܕܒܚܘܠܐ ܕܢܘܗܪܗ ܡܢ ܟܘܟܒܐ ܗ̄ ܡܠܟܝܢ ܢܗܘܢ ܡܫܠܛܐ ܘܡܫܘܚ ܒܪ ܟܘܟܒܐ. ܐܬܬܩܝܡ ܪܩܝܥܐ ܥܠ ܦܪܐ ܘܗܘܐ ܪܩܝܥܐ ܡܫܘܚܐ ܕܝܘܡܐ. ܘܐܬܦܪܫܘ ܦܘܠܓ̈ܐ ܘܠܡܫܠܛܢܘܬܐ ܕܪܩܝܥܐ ܗܢܝܢ ܐܝܬܝܗܝܢ ܡܫܘܚܐ ܕܒ̈ܢܝ ܦܘܠ̈ܓܐ ܕܡܫܬܟܠܠܝܢ ܥܕܡܐ ܠܥܠܡ ❖

ܫܠܡ

47 Ms erroneously ܠܗܘܡܐ (Brock).

[Colophon]

Written by the hands of someone weak and a sinner, named Kashisho Yuhanon of Pediekal, a member of the Ramamangalam parish, who is from the Syrian community of the Knanaites, from the Jacobite nation of the Christian religion, on 24th Elul (= September), 1915 of the Christian Era. In the church of North Paraur, when he was visitor, or fellow worker (Assistant Vicar), of the church in the name of the Holy Apostle Mar Thoma, Preacher of India.

ܠܒ̈ܢܝ ܐ̱ܢܫ ܕܗܘܐ ܘܣܠܩܐ ܕܫܡܫܗ ܫܡܫܐ ܡܫܝܚ ܕܒܗ ܫܒ̈ܝܚܬܐ ܠܗ:
ܡܒܪܟܬܐ ܕܐܬܒܣܡܬ ܗܘ ܕܐܠܗܐ ܡܢ ܫܘܫܠܬܐ ܕܫܘܩܝܐ ܫܠܝܚܐ ܠܝܚܢܐ
ܘܡܚܩܒܠܐ ܠܐܘܪܫܠܡ ܘܒܪܫܟܪܘܬܐ: ܒܗܘܢ ܩܒ ܠܐܡܬܘܠ ܒܡܢܗ ܐܪܝܡܗ
ܡܥܝܢܝܬܐ: ܒܒܝܬܐ ܕܦ̈ܪܘܣ ܒܪܒܝܬܐ: ܒܗ ܗܘ ܐܠܗܐ ܕܗܘܐ ܡܥܡܪܐ ܡܒܝܬܐ
ܕܗܘ ܒܒܝܬܐ ܕܒܫܡ ܡܪܢ ܠܐܘܡܬܐ ܡܠܟܝܢܐ ܡܢܝܐ ܒܪܘܪܘܬܗ.

✠✠✠✠✠

BIBLIOGRAPHY

ABBELOOS, J.B and LAMY T.J., *Gregorii Barhebraei Chronicon Ecclesiasticum*, 3 Vols., Louvain, 1872–1877.

APHRAM I, Patriarch Ignatius Barsoum, *The History of Syriac Literature and Sciences*, (tr. Matti Moosa, Pueblo, 2000.

ASSEMANI, S.J., *Bibliotheca Orientalis Clementino-Vaticana*, 4 Vols. Rome, 1719–1728.

BROCK, S., "The Thrice-holy hymn in the liturgy", *SOBORNOST/Eastern Churches Quarterly*, (1986), 24–34.

EBIED, Rifaat & Archbishop Malki Malki, "Patriarch Ignatius Bar Wahib's (d.1333) treatise on the six Syriac letters that have two sounds", *The Harp* 32 (2017), 9–37.

KONAT, Abraham (ed), *Ktobo d-slutho shhimto*, Pampakuda, 1968, 3rd edn.

VARGHESE, B. (tr), *The Commentary of Dionysius Bar Salibi on the Eucharist*, SEERI/ Gorgias Press, 2011.

VARGHESE, B. (tr), *Book of Guides (Hudaya) or Nomocanon by Gregorios Bar Hebraeus*, MOC Publications, Kottayam, 2014.

VARGHESE, B (ed & tr), *Order of the Anaphoras*, MOC Publications, 2021.

WILMSHURST, David (ed. & tr), *Bar Hebraeus. The Ecclesiastical Chronicle*, Gorgias Press, 2016.

www.ingramcontent.com/pod-product-compliance
Lightning Source LLC
Chambersburg PA
CBHW061420300426
44114CB00015B/2012